MAN SKILLS

Be Warned

A number of the entries in this book are highly dangerous and should only ever be approached with extreme caution. For example, while *Man Skills* suggests how best to jump from a speeding train or escape from a shark, these are to be used only as last resorts when all other hope has left the building. Only if you're a trained expert should you attempt any skill where your life is put in danger. The information contained in these pages is correct to the best of the author and publisher's knowledge and backed up by experts, but there are just too many variables to cover every situation. If you go out of your way to wrestle sharks, for example, based on the advice on page 153, you'll almost certainly get everything you deserve.

So, just to reiterate, we – the author, all experts involved, the publishers and everyone we know – disclaim any responsibility from any injury or death that may occur from following the guidance in this book. Equally, none of the skills here should be used to break any laws or infringe on the rights of any other person or persons.

Behave yourselves; be nice to each other and everything should be just fine.

Nick Harper

MAN SKILLS

A Training Manual for Men

NICK HARPER

Michael O'Mara Books Limited

First published in Great Britain in 2006 by
Michael O'Mara Books Limited
9 Lion Yard
Tremadoc Road
London SW4 7NQ

ISBN (10-digit): 1-84317-230-5
ISBN (13-digit): 978-1-84317-230-7

10 9 8 7 6 5 4 3 2

www.mombooks.com

Designed and typeset by Envy Design
Printed and bound in Great Britain by Clays Ltd, St Ives plc

Contents

Acknowledgements

Humble thanks, in no particular order, to Mark Pitt, Mike Glendinning, Phil and Jayne, Ben and Karen, Matt and Mel, Ian Quest, Dan Jones, Richard and Tanya, Simon Weeden, Ma and Pa Harper and Burdett, Lawrence and Fiona, Scott Murray, Dan Rookwood, Rob Smyth, Simon 'Dogs' Burdett and Muneni, Matt Pool, Boris, Toby Potter, Tom Goss, Chris and Claire, Michael Powell, all at MOM (particularly Chris and Lindsay), David Woodroffe, Al, Peaches, Mooro and Ollie, who sorted it

Most thanks of all to Sarah, for the many years of patience

And no thanks to Barry Glendenning, who was no help whatsoever

The Experts:
Champagne and Wine entries Bon Vivant Harry Putt (www.winefoodacademy.com)

Survive in Prison Peter Harper, Prison Officer, Buckley Hall Prison

Dive Like Tarzan Rob 'Frenchy' French, Playboy Lifeguard

Heimlich, Kiss of Life, Bleeding and Burns Joe Mulligan, Head of First Aid Services, Red Cross

Shake Hands Properly Thomas Blaikie, author of *Blaikie's Guide To Modern Manners* (Fourth Estate, 2005)

Deliver a Baby Virginia Howes, Independent Midwife (www.kentmidwiferypractice.co.uk)

All Car and Driving Skills Alan 'AJ' Jeffrey, Former Rally Driver and Technical Author

Catch a Fish with String Patrick McGlinchey, Survival Expert (www.backwoodssurvival.co.uk)

Pull Your Own Tooth 'No, Don't' – Dr Martin S. Spiller, Responsible Dentist

Hit the Hammer Thing Paul Jose of Fun Time Hire, Hammer Expert

Take a Punch Jezz Wilcox, Personal Trainer (www.thethirdspace.com)

Dance Moves Brent Ingleton, Club Moves Instructor (www.danceworks.net); mental tips: Jacqueline Butler, Dance Instructor

Jump from a Speeding Train Jon Epstein, Chuck Norris's stunt double

Mow the Lawn Mick Hunt, Head Groundsman, Lord's Cricket Club

Throw Like a Man Patrick Fallis, Cricket Coach
(www.coachingcricketexcellence.co.uk)

Buy Flowers Samantha Bayton, Flowergram Ltd
(www.flowergram.co.uk)

Mix a Cocktail Juha Kaskinen, Founder of London's
Cocktail Academy (www.cocktailacademy.co.uk)

Best Man Speech Advice and pointers courtesy of
www.lastnightoffreedom.co.uk

Buy a Suit Advice courtesy of www.suitmaker.co.uk

Cut-Throat Razor Advice courtesy of www.executive-
shaving.co.uk

Wash the Windows Tony Glendinning, Window Cleaner

Break Down Door and Fireman's Lift Tony Glendinning,
Fireman. (Yes, that's right, he's both.)

Second-Hand Car Greg Mills, Car Salesman

Arm Wrestle Neil Pickup, Twice European and World
Middleweight Arm-Wrestling Champion

Make Bow and Arrow Pete Davidson, Longbow Expert
(www.tradlongbows.co.uk)

Fire Bow and Arrow Mark Davis, Archery Instructor
(www.aasinfo.demon.co.uk)

Toss a Caber, Rip a Phone Book and Fairground Hammer
Geoff Capes, Athlete, Strongman and Prize-Winning
Budgerigar Breeder

HOW DID IT COME TO THIS?

I managed to get away with being hapless for the best part of thirty years – and I would probably have got away with it for much longer had my pesky father-in-law not rumbled me one Sunday morning late last year.

Assisting me with a few routine DIY tasks around the house I'd just moved into, he suggested I bleed the radiator while he set about plumbing in the washing machine. His casual, matter-of-fact tone suggested that my task would present few problems; indeed, it implied that men bleed radiators for fun from the age of twelve onwards.

He soon knew better, thanks to my blank, gormless expression, and the fact I approached the task holding a hacksaw. The only reason he didn't say anything was because we both knew he didn't have to; he was well within his rights to assume his only daughter had married the village idiot's half-wit brother. Tragically, the more I thought about it, the more I realized that I'd reached almost thirty-two years of age without learning any of the most important, and basic, Man Skills.

Obviously I could send an e-mail, set the video for a fortnight on Wednesday and download music I'd never listen to, but life's proper skills, the ones most dads know? Nope, absolutely no idea. Happily – for me, at least – I know

I'm not alone. Nobody bothers to learn how to mow the lawn properly or steer through a skid any more, so almost every man I know is as hapless as wot I am. Or at least, as hapless as wot I *was*, because I've spent many months researching and writing the book you hold before you.

I'm not claiming I know every trick in the book. I don't, and I wouldn't fancy my chances of landing a light aircraft should the pilot pass out. But I *do* now have a far better understanding of how to wire a plug, carve a chicken and change a baby's nappy without him pissing in my eye. Plus, I finally know that you don't bleed a radiator with a hacksaw, and by the end of this book, so will you.

My father-in-law still thinks I'm a hapless moron though, but you can't have everything.

How To...
Wire A Plug

If you don't learn any other skill in the book, make sure you master this one; the most basic requirement of any man. Not only will it ensure your toaster, TV and Corby trouser press are all fully functional, but the combination of colourful wires and sharp tools gives the impression you're attempting something both delicate and dangerous. You're not, as it turns out, but no one else needs to know that.

To make life easier, most products these days come with a fully functioning plug already attached. Even so, knowing how to replace a damaged plug – or rewire one from scratch – should stand you in good stead when the need inevitably arises. Luckily, it's embarrassingly easy...

Step 1. If you remove the back of a household plug that's already attached to an electrical device you'll find a fuse (that silvery little tube thing, on the right), a strap, and a fat flex running into the bottom of the plug, inside which live three colourful conductors: Earth (coloured green/yellow), Live (brown) and Neutral (blue).

Step 2. If starting with a brand new plug, you'll need to measure the flex against the three terminals to determine how far down the outer insulation (its skin, if you will) you'll need to snip to allow the three wires inside to reach their relevant terminals – 4 cm is industry standard. With a sharp knife or wire cutters, very carefully trim away this outer covering, and then use a pair of wire strippers to remove the insulation covering the three wires, leaving around 1 cm of exposed metal core on each. Bend each wire back on itself to ensure a more comfortable fit into its terminal.

Step 3. Loosen the three terminal screws, and connect the correct wire into the correct terminal and tighten the screw again to hold the wire in place. The brown wire goes into the terminal with the fuse, the blue wire into the terminal marked N (Neutral) and the green/yellow into the top terminal, which should be the only one left if you've done it right. Finally, screw the strap into place to secure the flex, reattach the cover and tighten the centre screw to secure it. Plug in, switch on and bask in the warm glow of light/noise/crease-free trousers etc.!

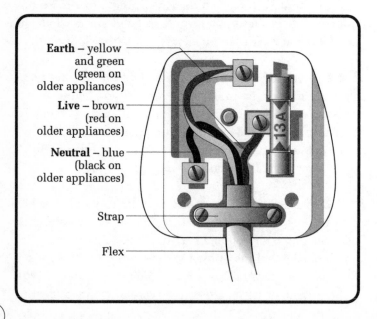

Earth – yellow and green (green on older appliances)

Live – brown (red on older appliances)

Neutral – blue (black on older appliances)

Strap

Flex

Step 4. (optional)

If you're merely replacing a damaged (normally cracked) plug, in most cases you won't need to trim down the flex. Simply unscrew the terminal screws and release the wire conductors, remove the strap holding in place the flex, pull out the flex, and reposition each component in the new plug, following closely the instructions above.

Warning: this advice applies only to British mains plugs and wiring. It doesn't cover the fiddly foreign ones.

How To ...
Shake Hands Properly

There's more to it than just clamping onto the other bloke's hand and holding on. Admittedly, not *much* more to it than that, but we wouldn't want you to make the wrong first impression and for him to think you're an oddball from the off, so follow the advice closely.

Shake a stranger's hand too firmly and he'll think you're trying to outmuscle him in a test of manhood that may later lead on to a bout of naked wrestling on the hearth. Shake too limply and he'll quite rightly dismiss you as a spineless cretin who's not to be trusted. The art is to find a happy balance, and the unwritten rules are simple ...

The perfect handshake

Make eye contact, smile, or say 'hello', and extend your right hand, held at a slight downward angle.

Your grip should be firm but never fierce – this is not a test of brute force so never *squeeze* his hand.

Shake using only your lower arm, and never bring your shoulder into play – that's when it becomes more physical; he'll sniff testosterone.

Grip his hand for just two or three seconds, applying a couple of short, controlled shakes to convey sincerity. (Movement of the hand is actually optional in a handshake, but if you don't move it up and down you're merely holding a strange man's hand for a bit. If we lived in a more open, tolerant society that would be fine, but we don't.)

Maintain eye contact throughout the shake and until the hands are withdrawn.

Assuming all's gone to plan, he'll think you're the kind of stand-up character he could happily employ, grant his daughter's hand in marriage to or just share some booze and fine cigars with long into the night. Possibly all three, if you've pulled off a really great shake.

The golden rules

- One handshake should fit all occasions: don't go changing it to suit different surroundings and people.
- The only time you should alter your approach is when shaking a woman's hand. Even then, simply lighten the grip slightly so as to not come across as some kind of frenzied sex pest.
- The two-handed shake is a nice touch, but 'a bit too familiar' for strangers. Save it for close friends and long-time associates only.
- Hold on too long and the other person will think you're particularly needy.
- But never snatch your hand back; that's just rude.
- Keep your body language open throughout the shake.
- Make sure your hands are dry.
- Never fidget as you shake.
- Don't wink, unless you're a cocky wanker.
- And never use the comedy hand-buzzer gag on strangers. Save it for your 'wacky' pals.

How To ...
Buy Flowers

This is stupidly complicated, so concentrate a bit harder here.

The flowers you buy a woman have to be the right model for the right occasion. You might think wilting daffodils from the petrol station or half a dozen cheap roses from the tinker at the traffic lights will suffice, but according to the mind-bogglingly complex Flower Rules For Men, you'd be very wrong indeed. Having seen a tatty photocopy of these Rules, the following is a manly stab at making sense of it all ...

Surprise her

If you only ever buy her flowers when you've done something wrong or want something unreasonable from her, she'll associate them with guilt. Get in the habit of buying her flowers for no reason whatsoever and they'll mean a damn sight more.

Romance

You can always play it safe with a nice bunch of red roses on Valentine's Day, just to prove once and for all that you have no imagination whatsoever. Or you could go for azaleas, tulips, violets or bouquets of mixed flowers, which are all more imaginative and often less expensive. Not that money should be the issue where this special lady's concerned, of course.

Her birthday

You wouldn't want to get this wrong and ruin her big day, surely? If in doubt, a bouquet is your safest bet, and £35 is the approximate going rate for a decent bunch (at the time of going to press).

Your anniversary

If you married her, a good starting point is to first remember the correct date, then try to recall what flowers she had on her wedding day. You could scratch your chin for a while before plumping for the wrong thing. Or you could ask one of her bridesmaids, or just check your wedding photos to save time and money. A simple choice really.

Bad occasions

Good flowers for when bad stuff like deaths, amputations and redundancy happen include (but are not limited to) forget-me-nots, statice and hydrangea. They suggest you're in touch with your sensitive side, even if you're not.

Get well

No real hard or fast rules here, apart from to make sure that if you're sending flowers to someone in hospital that they're allowed to have them on the ward. Don't send tulips as they wilt in the heat. And black roses, Nemophila Penny Black or any other black flowers might convey the wrong sort of message.

New baby

According to The Rules, Gardenias = Joy = A Safe Bet.

Colour-coded (for extra confusion)

If you're comfortable with the above and want to pretend you know flowers on a deeper level, be aware that their colours signify different things.

Red flowers equal passion, love, fire and heat. Orange suggests fire and warmth, yellow is associated with spring, happiness and sunshine.

Blue flowers suggest peace, serenity and calm; purple equals luxury, splendour and Elton John-esque opulence, while pink shouts femininity and grace and all that girly stuff.

White flowers denote purity, light and innocence, while black, they claim, suggests style and enchantment (but also 'impending death' if delivered to an ailing pensioner).

If in doubt, go for her favourite colour, or something that matches the colour of the room they're likely to be left to wither in.

And if you only read one thing on this page ...

The most important of all Flower Rules For Men is: if in doubt, ask the nice lady behind the counter. As a woman, she'll happily bang on at great length and will always know far more than you. Tell her the occasion, she'll work out all the complicated sub-texts and send you off with the right bunch.

How To...
Carve A Chicken Like A Pro

(Or if you'd prefer, a turkey, for the technique is exactly the same.)

Hack away at the fowl aimlessly and you'll be left with a shabby little pile of scrag-ends that you'd think twice about feeding a cat. Carve in the measured manner detailed below and you'll end up with fat slices of prime white poultry and several arched eyebrows ...

Once cooked, take the bird out of the oven and let it rest, breast-side up, for at least fifteen minutes. This allows the fibres to relax, which makes carving through its flesh far easier, and which in turn clearly makes you look like you know what you're doing. Use a cutting board with a little trough round the edge so when you cut into the chicken its precious, tasty juices aren't wasted.

Once it has rested take one very sharp, very flexible, thin-bladed carving knife, and a two-pronged carving fork (to steady the bird), and chop it up like so ...

Step 1. Cut down between the leg and the breast. Pull the thigh away from the bird and cut through the joint to remove this choice dark meat – attempt to cut through the bone and you'll be there all day.

Step 2. To separate thigh from drumstick (the meat around the leg bone), cut through the ball and socket joint, then remove the opposite leg in a similar fashion. As a general rule, never buy a chicken if it has fewer or more than two legs.

Step 3. Before you can carve the big bits off the breast, make sure you remove the wishbone, otherwise it'll only get in the way and make things harder. To do this, loosen the skin from the flesh at the neck with your fingers, folding back the skin to expose the breastbone (the big bone that runs along the middle of the front). You should now be able to whip out that wishbone with a minimum of fuss.

Wishbone

Step 4. Cut horizontally above the wing joint and along through the breast – this makes it much easier to carve off the big juicy showpiece slices of meat in one.

Step 5. Finally, carve downwards and parallel to the breastbone, going in as close to the bone as possible so as not to waste any precious meat. Repeat on the other side of the bone until you're left with a stripped carcass. Share the meat out amongst your hungry guests, serving with some roast potatoes and perhaps a nice dribble of gravy.

How To ...
Undo A Bra Using Only One Hand

In the hands of a randy novice, bra straps can maim and possibly even kill. That's not merely scaremongering for the purpose of a more dramatic introduction – it's based on the sorry tale of a young man who needed plastic surgery after catching a finger in the bra of his busty companion.

He was twenty-seven and knew no better (though certainly should have done by that age), and his injuries were serious enough for surgeons to suggest the introduction of Bra Camps for naive young men. Well, kind of. '[We] advocate patient self-education (during the adolescent years) on the mechanism of external female mammary support and postulate that it may be important in reducing the incidence of other such injuries,' claimed the *British Journal of Plastic Surgeons* in 2002.

Sadly, Bra Camps have not been forthcoming, and because you're attempting to unhook the external female mammary support with just the *one* hand, the following guide may just save your life ...

Step 1. Along with a series of small hooks, tension in the bra strap keeps the garment tight – you'll need to isolate that tension before you can whip the bra clean off. Having slid your hand casually round her back, place thumb and fore-finger on the top, outer side of the bra strap, on either side of the locked hooks, with your three remaining fingers sliding underneath the bra strap.

Step 2. The three fingers should isolate the tension in the strap by pulling it away slightly from the woman's back, with the thumb and forefinger gently squeezing together to release the hooks.

Step 3. If done properly, you should still be injury-free, the unhooked straps should fall down and the bra will be hanging free. If you need tips on what to do next, you'll need to buy a mucky book. That one with the bearded man on the front comes highly recommended.

How To...
Start A Fire With Two Sticks

To be honest, where it says 'Two Sticks', it should probably read 'A Stick, A Stone, A Large Piece Of Board, Some Tinder, Another Stick And A Sore Arm', only that's not quite as snappy. This trick is also known as the bow and drill method, a moniker that would have also seen you reaching for the next page, so let's go with the Two Sticks. This technique has been made popular of late by portly bush warrior Ray Mears. It takes an age to prepare and an eternity to perfect, but apart from that it's a simple way of making an impressive Big Fire. This handy illustration shows the components involved ...

The socket – an easy-to-grasp stone or piece of hardwood with a small indent in the centre of the underside to hold the drill in place as you apply downward pressure.

The drill – this needs to be a straight, robust stick roughly 2 cm in diameter and about 20 cm long. The top end should be rounded, enabling it to fit snugly into the socket's indent, and the bottom end must be more pointed to generate more friction.

The fireboard – this can be any size you like, though a seasoned (dried) softwood board at least 5 cm wide, 15 cm long and 2 cm thick is the preferred choice of most bushmen. You'll need to cut a depression close to the edge on one side of the board, big enough to accommodate the bottom of the drill. On the underside, whittle a V-shaped cut from the edge of the board to the depression (see illustration). This V-shaped notch should cut a small hole into the base of the depression, just big enough to allow the powder you'll produce to drop through to the tinder (see the illustration again, and look very closely). We're getting ahead of ourselves here. Keep concentrating hard and read on.

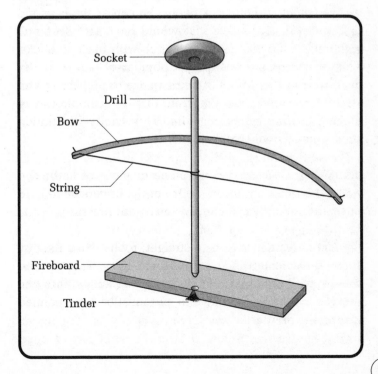

The bow – this needs to be about 2.5 cm in diameter, and robust enough not to snap the moment you tie string to either end and bend it into shape. Simply cut a notch at either end of the stick, about an inch or so deep. Feed string through one notch and fasten with a knot, then bend the wood into a bow shape and secure with a second knot. Tie tight enough for the stick to stay bent.

After constructing the bow and drill, but before you begin the funny sawing motion, you'll need to collect a nice big pile of wood and kindling – if, after all your exertions, you end up with a flame but no wood to burn, you're more stupid than you look. (See page 145, How To … Build A Fire.)

Now, shove a bundle of finely-shredded tinder (which can be dead grass, leaves – anything dry, that will burn) under the V-shaped cut in the fireboard, place one foot firmly on the board to keep it steady, then loop the bow-string over the drill shaft (see illustration), making sure the tension is firm. Position the drill in the pre-cut depression in the board, place the socket on top, held down with one hand, and you're all set.

Press down on the drill and move the bow from side to side using a steady horizontal sawing motion. As the motion becomes smoother, apply more downward pressure on the socket and work the bow faster. Saw as fast as your fat little fingers will go, then a bit faster still.

Eventually, after what may well seem like four days of this repetitive and tedious exertion, your sawing motion should grind the wood into a hot black powder. When the powder falls down onto the tinder, the heat should eventually provide a spark. Blow gently on the tinder until it ignites, and protect it from the wind as you move it towards your pre-prepared fire. Introduce it to the fire's kindling (dry twigs and leaves) and nurture until it rages nicely. The feeling should return to your arm after a few hours, and you should get faster with practice.

An alternative method for making a fire

The convex lens method won't make your hands bleed and requires you only to lie still for a while. It's only an option on a bright, sunny day, and you'll need the lens on a pair of binoculars, a camera or a magnifying glass for it to work. Angle said lens so that it directs the sun's rays on to a small pile of tinder. Hold in place until the tinder starts to smoulder and gently blow on it to turn tinder into flame. Apply it to your pre-prepared fire and wonder why you ever bothered making fire with two sticks.

How To...
Beat A Hangover

When you finally wake up in a pool of stagnant dribble, your head will be pounding and you'll stink of cheap booze and smoke. If you have work today, you're in trouble, not to mention late. If it's the weekend and you're free to sit around all day in your pants, you'll still want to shake the bastard behind your eyes as quickly as possible. Before detailing The Miracle Cure, however, a brief scientific explanation as to why you're feeling so shoddy. (Not that you'll care at this moment...)

Brief scientific explanation
It's either the cogeners (impurities) in your alcohol or it's the ethanol, a toxic fug coughed up by your liver as it breaks down the booze. Either way, you're buggered, so best we skip the bit about vasopressin and methanol and head straight onto The Miracle Cure ...

The Miracle Cure
Sorry, we've just checked again and there is no miracle cure. The only way to avoid a hangover is to drink in moderation or abstain completely, neither of which are any fun at all. Alternatively, you could continually top up your alcohol levels, thereby keeping one step ahead of the hangover, but a book as responsible as this would advise

against that. So, your only hope is to limit the damage as much as possible.

Before you start boozing

Eat fatty food and drink milk to line your stomach. This slows the absorption of booze into your bloodstream, giving your body time to process the toxins in the grog more effectively.

If you can limit yourself to one drink per hour, your body should be able to process the alcohol and keep you on an even keel. One. Per hour. And even then this is based on quaffing 3 to 4 per cent Sports Lagers. Any of the 5 per cent-plus big-hitting premium ales will make a mockery of this advice.

The darker the drink, the greater the chance of you waking up with a throbbing head. Cogeners give drinks their different colours and tastes, but as toxins they also poison your body and leave you in a sorry heap.

And never mix your drinks, particularly not the dark ones. Toxins combined gang up to do far more damage.

Sup water between drinks, even if it's on the sly in the toilet. Alcohol is a diuretic, which means your body will make you piss out every last drop of water instead of sending it to the various vital organs that need water to function properly. Deprived of water, your brain will shrink and you'll wake up feeling like death.

Fizzy drinks may seem a wise option as a 'top' on your lager or a good glug of tonic in your short, but they're not. They've been scientifically proven to speed up the alcohol absorption into your system, plus they rot your teeth and make you flabby.

As a rule, bottled beer has higher alcohol content than pints, primarily because the landlord can't get at it to water it down and make it go further. Not all landlords do this, just the unscrupulous bastards. And they know who they are.

And when you stagger in with sick in your hair and chilli sauce down your front, remember to drink yet more water before passing out in a heap. It will help rehydrate you, although you're still going to feel like shit in about four hours ...

The next day [about four hours later]

Having ignored all of the above, you wake up feeling like shit. Your only hope now is to hope one of the following 'hangover cures' actually works. You have nothing to lose ...

Sleep As long as possible. It might go away.

Vitamins A, B and C The body loses all three as you guzzle booze. Replace in tablet or food forms as soon as possible. Vitamin A is found in eggs and carrots, B in bananas and chilli peppers and C in all good citrus fruits.

Coffee or Cola Caffeine helps reduce the swelling of blood vessels in your brain, although it will also dehydrate you and make matters worse unless you glug water as well.

A canary According to the ancient Romans (who knew a thing or two about debauchery), a canary for breakfast works wonders. They'd fry him, probably in olive oil, although grilling is considered far healthier.

Ginger Grated into orange juice or taken in pill form, this has been known to work well on dodgy stomachs.

Chocolate Your body uses up its sugar supply breaking down the booze. You'll need to replace it asap.

Exercise Jumping up and down helps send blood and oxygen to your shrivelled brain, while the sweat flushes the toxins out of your body. Sex also helps, apparently.

Half a lemon According to Puerto Rican booze fans, if you rub the halved lemon under your drinking arm you'll be feeling fiddle-fit within the hour.

Burnt toast The carbon is good for soaking up the poisonous toxins floating around your body, although it tastes shit.

Bananas Contain magnesium, potassium and sugar, which are lost as you drink.

Raw cabbage Helps cure a headache. Germans swear by sauerkraut juice to replace lost nutrients.

Menudo soup The Mexican alternative, available in a can and containing tripe, dried maize and pigs' feet. Yes, coughing your guts up can also make you feel better.

Take one or more of the above, lie down with the curtains closed and wait for the room to settle. Keep waiting and eventually you'll feel better, then you'll accept that you're getting older and can't shake it off like you used to. You'll tell yourself that booze abuse is a young man's game and vow never to imbibe so greedily ever again. You can shake your head all you like though, because you're fooling no one.

How To ...
Crack Open A Coconut

You're right, clanking it against a sturdy wall or brick would do the job, but such a ham-fisted approach would guarantee most of the lovely juice inside the nut is wasted. So, this technique is for the controlled, idiot-proof approach ...

Step 1. Rest the coconut in the middle of one hand, with the tip at one end and the 'eyes' at the other. If you have a bowl to hand, hold the coconut over it to catch the juice.

Step 2. Find a blunt implement – the back of a knife or a stout stone – and bang the coconut around its centre, rotating the seed until it gently starts to split open. As the crack widens, pour the juice into your bowl or straight down your trap. Once the juice has drained, to get to the flesh continue knocking at the coconut shell until it opens. You should be left with two even halves, but no one's measuring.

Step 3. To reach the juice without splitting the nut open, hammer a sharp tip into the 'eyes' of the nut – a nail or sharp stone should suffice. Insert a straw and you've turned that coconut into a tall drink to be sipped at leisure. If you've been washed up on a deserted island, however, you may struggle for a straw so should skip this final step altogether.

How To ...
Master The Fireman's
Lift (And Carry)

Britain's firefighters are the best in the world and they do a marvellous job, gawd bless 'em, and so on and so forth. However, it's impossible to expect them to be on hand at the start of every emergency. Sometimes they're otherwise engaged drinking tea or putting out a small bin fire, which is why you may need to know how to cart someone to safety in the unlikely event of a fire.

The victim here has been overcome by the smoke and fumes or is just too injured to hobble to safety after a large pot of glue landed awkwardly on their leg during the commotion, or what have you. You're first on the scene and have just read the following instructions ...

The lift and carry

The lift is easier if you have an accomplice to help pick him (or her) up. However, assuming you don't, you'll need to struggle the victim up and onto his feet as best you can. He (we'll assume) should be facing you, with your right leg bent at the knee and advanced between his thighs, with your weight on that front foot.

With his weight resting on your right thigh, grip the victim's right hand with your left and place your right arm under his crotch and round the back of his right thigh (see figure 1). If you're playing the hero by rescuing a woman, your hand should go around the outside and rear of her thighs, in case she wakes up and finds you fumbling around near her parts.

Bending at the knees and using his right arm as a lever, pull the victim up and over your 'leading' shoulder, distributing his weight as evenly as possible and using your legs to bear the weight to avoid twanging your back. Be aware that it's only a proper fireman's carry if the victim is carried across both shoulders – dispersing their weight will let you carry them further and with minimum disruption to their potentially injured body.

Stand as tall as possible, bending your head forwards slightly to minimize your discomfort (figure 2), and slowly stagger off to somewhere safer, like over there.

Fig. 1   Fig. 2

Taking sides

If you've gone that extra yard by clambering heroically up a ladder and through a window to save your victim, the side of the window your ladder is resting on determines over which shoulder you carry the person. If you're right-handed, you'll naturally favour your right shoulder for bearing the brunt of the weight, so should therefore pitch your ladder alongside the right of the window. This ensures the victim's head is less likely to clank violently against the window frame as you clamber back out. If your ladder is pitched on the left, remember to adjust these instructions accordingly – and whichever side you approach from, take good care on the way back down.

How To ...
Bleed A Radiator

An expert on this kind of thing would advise you to bleed your radiators at least twice a year, then when you ignore their advice charge you £125 to fix them and only accept cash-in-hand.

Thanks to this entry, you'll now be able to tell him where to stick his hourly rate and bleed it yourself, for it's a stupidly simple procedure. For 'bleed the radiator', read 'drain your central heating system of any air that's made its way in.'

Air in your heating system is a common problem and nothing to be ashamed about. As you heat and cool water, air bubbles are released. That air rises to the highest part of the heating system – normally your radiator – and displaces some of the water, and because air doesn't conduct heat anywhere near as efficiently as water you'll soon notice the difference in temperature. Left inside, the air will dramatically reduce the amount of heat your radiator emits until one day you wake to find an Eskimo catching fish at the end of your bed.

The telltale sign of when a radiator needs bleeding is if, when the heating is on, the top part is noticeably colder than the bottom – this suggests there's a little air trapped inside. If it's cool from top to bottom, you've just got a lot more air to bleed dry. That's the science bit over, here's how you bleed ...

Step 1. Turn the central heating off at the thermostat and allow the water to cool. Then, insert a bleed key into the bleed valve – which is the little screwy nub thing normally located at the top end of the radiator, or sometimes round the back. Before turning the key, wrap an old rag around it to catch any dirty water which might spurt out onto the carpet, or on those smart new slacks of yours.

Step 2. Give the bleed valve a stout half-turn anti-clockwise until you hear a hissing sound – don't be overly alarmed, that's just the sound of the air escaping.

Step 3. When the hissing stops the air has escaped, at which point some dirty water should splurge out into the rag. That's your cue to close the valve by turning it back to its original position – a half-turn clockwise, should you be struggling to keep pace.

Step 4. Remove scarf and gloves, bask in the warmth of a job well done and make a note to do it again in six months' time.

How To ...
Communicate Using
Morse Code

Morse code was one of the earliest forms of text messaging, dreamt up by Samuel Morse in the 1830s to let his boss know he wouldn't be coming in today because he was coming down with flu although it turned out to be nothing more than a mild man-cold that soon passed but his boss didn't need to know that.

Still popular to this day among salty sea dogs, the twenty-six letters of the alphabet, the numbers 1 to 9, and various punctuation marks are broken down into a series of simple dots and dashes, traditionally transmitted by radio pulses.

For the man who rarely ventures out to sea, however, the code can just as easily be transmitted by torch light to your mate across the road, or to Mr Wong at Wok This Way. He doesn't deliver, of course, but I can't do anything about that.

The Code
A dot indicates a short pulse of light or sound, and a dash a longer one.

A . –	Z – – ..
B – ...	1 . – – – –
C – . – .	2 .. – – –
D – ..	3 ... – –
E .	4 .... –
F .. – .	5 .....
G – – .	6 – ....
H	7 – – ...
I ..	8 – – – ..
J . – – –	9 – – – – .
K – . –	0 – – – – –
L . – ..	Full stop . – . – . –
M – –	Comma – – .. – –
N – .	Colon – – – ...
O – – –	Question mark .. – – ..
P . – – .	Exclamation mark – . – . – –
Q – – . –	Apostrophe . – – – – .
R . – .	Hyphen – .... –
S ...	Fraction symbol – .. – .
T –	Quotation mark . – .. – .
U .. –	Equals sign – ... –
V ... –	Ignore the previous word (it
W . – –	was a mistake) .... (eight
X – .. –	dots)
Y – . – –	

The dash is normally three times as long as the dot. A word of warning though: be sure to leave a sufficient delay between transmitting each letter, otherwise it'll produce either a continuous, ear-splitting noise or a randomly flashing light, which may give the impression you're just having a party.

Sod the pigeon

The first successful transmission using Morse Code was on 6 January 1838, when Morse and his pioneering sidekick Alfred Vail sent a message three miles down a wire. It read:

.- / .-. - .- - .. . -. - / .-- .- .. - . .-. / .. ... /
-. --- / .-.. --- ... . .-. .-.-

Yes, you will have to work it out yourself. You've been taking *Man Skills* for granted.

How To ...
Give A Best Man's Speech

Unless you're some kind of social delinquent, at some point in your life you'll probably be asked to stand up and say a few kind words about a close friend and his newly wed wife. There's no right or wrong way to do this, but there are many ways of making a fool of yourself. The following pointers should steer you in the right direction ...

Tip 1. Fail to prepare ...

... and prepare to make a complete and utter arse of yourself in front of a room full of his and her (or her and her, or his and his) relatives. In the months leading up to the wedding, put together a loose skeleton of a speech, adding to it whenever you hear a half-decent anecdote that sounds about right, or you remember something from your childhood / school days / university life / et cetera that seems appropriate.

Eventually you'll have too many anecdotes, at which point you'll need to cast off the more unsavoury narratives and prepare a final speech. Ideally, you should do this a few weeks before the wedding, giving you time to perfect the structure. By all means add a few creative tweaks right up to the moment you stand up, but avoid any last-minute re-writes – this will only cause you confusion. And you can ill afford that.

Also, don't make the mistake of thinking you can turn up on the day and hit them with a little improv, effortlessly working the room like Dustin Gee in his prime. You can't, and you will die on your feet in a funny suit you've been made to wear.

Tip 2. Start as you mean to go on

Your opening gambit is crucial if you're to pull this off. There are three possible angles of approach ...

Safe-bet subjects

These include: the happy couple's unique magic ... the way they sparkle together ... all that kind of flowery balls the old people like ... talk about the groom's amusing childhood stories ... except any involving him discovering the magical powers of his front tail – that would be bad ... stick with complementing the 'marvellous venue' and the 'lovely food' ... compliment the bridesmaids, but don't leer or wink inappropriately ... in short, just say nice things about all the nice people and offend nobody.

Thin-ice subjects

Talk about how the couple first met, providing he didn't have her shipped over from Bangkok in a box ... mention the groom's embarrassing habits, but keep them of the non-genital variety ... and look ahead to the honeymoon, that should be safe enough, you'd think ...

Ice breakers

Don't mention what really went on at the stag weekend or produce photographic evidence and receipts to back up your claims ... don't discuss his or her previous partners and all the stuff they got up to ... don't, at any point, start a sentence with the phrase: 'My mother-in-law ...' ... say nothing negative about the food or the venue, even if they offered very poor value for money ... and don't rank the bridesmaids, at least not out loud ...

Tip 3. The delivery

Tragically, the tone and delivery you're looking for is the Hugh Grant character in loveable Brit flick *Four Weddings and a Funeral* – inoffensive charm delivered by a floppy-haired, upper-crust buffoon. Choose your content wisely, then follow these simple pointers:

- Prompt cards are fine, though anything over A3 might be a bit excessive.
- A good length for the speech depends on what's gone before it. You'll be delivering your speech after the groom's brief introduction and the bride's father's drunken ramble, so judge how long it should run for. If they've both blathered on at length you may need to trim yours down as you go, as people can only feign attention for so long. If they both nervously whipped through theirs in double-quick time, you may be better off adding an extra anecdote or two – the crowd will want their money's worth even if they didn't pay to get in.
- Avoid excess alcohol before the speeches. A little Dutch courage is fine, a pie-eyed pissant with soup down his front is less fine.
- Work the crowd by maintaining eye contact and sweeping the room. This projects confidence, even if you're so nervous you could well touch cloth.
- To keep the tone lively, try to inflect some form of

expression in your voice, particularly at the start and end of each line. A monotone delivery will have people reaching for the gin.

- Be yourself and avoid the pompous little touches you think the event demands – leave all that 'Lords, Ladies and Gentlemen' cobblers at home. Use your natural speaking voice and normal mannerisms, and remember that the groom picked you because of who you are rather than who you can pretend to be. Impersonations of famous people are ill-advised, unless you can do them really well. Even then, it's questionable. No one likes a smug tit, or indeed an impressionist.

- Visual gimmickry can help keep people's attention while they're drinking themselves into a light stupor. An amusing poster or suitable item of clothing can both work, a PowerPoint presentation is inexcusable.

- Avoid in-jokes, unless you want to lose 98 per cent of the guests when you ramble on about badger-baiting in Soho.

- Most important of all, remember that the vast majority of the crowd don't want you to make a complete arse of yourself. Hear them laugh at things which aren't even remotely funny and you'll realize they want you to do well. Why, they admire your balls for getting up in the first place and have no idea that you drunkenly begged the groom to get someone else to do it. Ah well, it's too late now. Just get up there, do your thing, then you can drink until you can no longer see.

How To...
Hit A Fairground
Hammer
(And Make The Bell Ring)

No self-respecting fairground should be allowed to open its gates without first having installed one of those test-of-strength hammer contraptions, and no self-respecting male should be allowed to visit a fairground without knowing how to make the weight scuttle up the pin and make the bell ring. With the world's smallest goldfish riding on it, failure is not an option.

The uninitiated man normally attempts to hit the target with all the might he can muster, not unreasonably thinking that raw power will bring success. But as his veins bulge, his hands blister and the weight climbs all of 10 centimetres, this man can only shuffle off shamefaced, muttering under his breath about the tinkers having rigged the machine.

The skilled man understands that the difference between success and failure here is not brute force, but hand-eye co-ordination. A weak man who hits the target flush stands a far better chance of ringing the bell than a muscular freak who lands his hammer hard on the edge of the target.

If you're in any position to practise, trade power for

accuracy until your eye is 'in', then concentrate on applying as much power and speed through the swing as your frame allows, without ever ceding accuracy. Swing over your shoulder or round your waist, whichever allows for a better strike.

To separate the men from the boys, some fairgrounds use longer pins, which require a more powerful blow to send the weight scuttling up to the top. Your best bet here is to prepare by working on your biceps and bulking up on powdered whey so that your neck thickens and your genitals shrivel. Or alternatively, know when you're beaten and try the coconut shy instead. (In which case, see page 161, How To ... Throw Properly.)

How To ...
Drink A Yard Of Ale

If you're a fan of binge drinking – and these days, who isn't? – then you'll want to do it properly by quaffing four pints of suspiciously cloudy brown ale from a long glassy shaft in one swift tip.

The Yard of Ale has been around since at least 1685, when noted English scribe John Evelyn wrote about 'his Majesty's health being drunk in a flint glass of a yard long'. If his majesty himself took part in such debauched revelry it isn't recorded, but the act quickly caught on among stagecoach drivers, back when horse-drawn carriages were the quickest means of travel. So bone-idle that they couldn't be bothered to climb down from their seat above the carriage, the yard glass could be passed straight up to them. They drained it in one, started up the horses and wheel-spinned away, often careering off into crowds of innocent peasants.

Most recently of all, as this limited history draws to a close, the Yard of Ale was made popular by rugby types who cottoned onto the fact that the only way to enjoy booze is by drinking copiously with your trousers round your ankles and a cream cracker stuck between your arse-cheeks. Best we conveniently ignore that fact and press on with the instructions ...

The instructions

The obvious problem is that your gullet wasn't designed to down four pints of booze in one hearty swig, so you'll end up drinking ale through both nostrils until you master the technique. Luckily, it's not all that difficult. All you need to be aware of is the infamous 'air rush'. This occurs when you tip the vessel up as you drink – the displaced booze is replaced by an air pocket which rushes down to the bottom of the yard and forces the remaining ale down the flute and towards your gullet at great speed. This can be prevented by using one of two fool-proof techniques.

Technique 1. The simplest of the two is to ignore the baying crowd and drink slowly but surely. Tilt the glass very, very steadily until it's emptied to the point where air can enter slowly and safely – thus avoiding that air rush. Your manhood will be questioned if you're still drinking twenty minutes later, but at least your slacks will stay dry.

Technique 2. The second option is far more of a crowd-pleaser. Drain the yard as normal, but give the impression you're a seasoned pro by slowly twirling the glass in a clockwise direction once you reach the bulb. Because the twisting motion releases the air pressure gently, you'll again avoid that late wave and reach the end unscathed. With experience, you'll be able to tilt the shaft more sharply, allowing you to finish your yard in a better time.

For now, raise your hand in triumph, wipe the suds from your chin and try not to vomit down your leg.

Speed supping

According to the book of *Guinness World Records*, the fastest recorded gulping of a Yard of Ale was by Northants-based boozer Peter Dowdeswell. He drank his 1.42 litres (just 2.5 pints, mind) in 5 seconds on 4 May 1975. In 1955, while a Rhodes scholar at University College, Oxford, Australian Prime-Minister-to-be Bob Hawke set the standard for his countrymen by necking the same volume of subsidized ale in 11 seconds, putting himself in the *Guinness World Records* book at the same time. And all at the taxpayer's expense. Ripper.

How To...
Tie A Bow Tie

Let's assume, for argument's sake, that at some point in your life you'll move in the type of circles where a bow tie is required. Now you could always buy a clip-on and save yourself the bother of reading this next page and of tying yourself in knots, but clip-ons are for charlatans and buffoons. Do it properly, like so ...

Step 1. Here's a nice looking bow tie, drawn as you'd see it in the mirror. The left end, as you see it, should be about 4 cm lower than the right end.

Step 2. Cross the longer length over the shorter end.

Step 3. Feed the longer end up through the loop.

Step 4. Now, take the shorter end and form the front loop of your bow by doubling it up and placing it across your shirt's collar points (the pointy bits on your, erm, collar).

Step 5. Holding that front loop with the thumb and forefinger of your left hand, allow the long end to drop down over the front. You'll notice that this baby's almost effortlessly taking shape now.

Step 6. Holding it all in place, double the long end back on itself. Poke that long end through the loop behind the tie, even up the ends and tighten.

Step 7. You're all done. You'll look even smarter when you put some trousers on.

How To ...
Mow The Lawn

Lawn mowing gets a bad press, and rightly so – it's a tedious pain in the arse and it gobbles up your weekend. So, the following ten tips have been cobbled together to help make the whole process as painless as possible. They won't win you any horticultural awards but at least you'll have a nice, greenish patch of grass to sit on should the sun ever bother to show its face ...

Tip 1. Buy a decent cylinder mower, preferably one with a box to catch the clippings, which will take the strain off your back. Cylinder mowers give more distinct and lasting strips and are good for cutting those fancy football-pitch stripes all men admire. Keep the blades sharp at all times for a cleaner cut.

Tip 2. If you've allowed it to become a shabby, overgrown garden, prod a big stick into the undergrowth before you begin to make sure there are no rocks or moles hiding in there. Both will mangle the blades on your new mower, and you won't be able to take it back because you've already lost the receipt.

Tip 3. Always cut an overgrown garden down in stages. This allows the roots to recover between cuts. Lop it off in one go and they'll weaken, go into shock and whimper a bit before dying on you – and then it really will look shabby. Also, never make the mistake of thinking that if you buzz the lawn as low as it can go, you won't have to cut it so soon again next time – you'll be pulling the roots too close to the surface and exposing them to damaging sunlight.

Tip 4. How low should you go? Good question. This varies, depending on how much it rains and how fast the grass grows and what have you, but a general guide is just over a centimetre in the summer to 2 centimetres in winter. If kids and dogs are likely to trample on it, keep the grass a little longer to protect it from wear and tear. If you only plan to read the papers out there on a Sunday morning, you can afford to take it down a little more. But be warned: a proper expert who knows what he's talking about would tell you that cutting more than one-third of the height of the grass in any one session will seriously damage those precious roots.

Tip 5. To make your lawn look as healthy as possible during the summer months, feed it a lawn fertilizer in late spring. Follow the instructions on the packet and expect greener, thicker turf that's free of weeds and moss.

Tip 6. During hot spells, let the grass grow a little longer and mow less often. Don't feed or water it, even if it starts to turn brownish – you'll encourage the grass to root closer to the surface, which can cause long-term damage in the fierce heat.

Tip 7. Never mow when the grass is wet or frosty. You won't get a good, even cut and are more likely to spread fungus about the turf.

Tip 8. When the conditions do finally allow you to mow, vary the direction to stop the grass getting lazy and leaning to one side after several cuts. A wonky lawn just looks shoddy, so keep the precious buggers on their toes.

Tip 9. A dirty great roller will flatten the grass, but if the ground is too compact the roots aren't able to move round as much as they need to, and that's a bad thing. A decent cylinder mower's built-in roller will do the job just fine.

Tip 10. Finally, when trimming edges, lay a plank of wood along the perimeter to give you a nice straight edge, and a thick, heavy rope along the edge of curvy borders. Use clippers on the edges for a more professional finish, or pressgang a young person into doing the job if you can no longer be bothered. Frankly, you deserve to put your feet up for a while.

How To...
Change A Baby's Nappy

Sadly, there's only so long you can ignore the noxious waft from a soiled nappy in the hope that it'll just go away. It won't, so you'll have to clean up the mess yourself for a change. A baby's through-put is nothing short of staggering – on average, he'll fill fifteen nappies to the brim every day and take pride in filling it back up again the minute you've changed him. The only saving grace is that the nappy changing is relatively easy if you're using disposables, so use these and conveniently ignore the fact they're not as environmentally friendly as cloth nappies (but then you don't have to wash them).

Mothers generally change nappies after a feed or when 'putting them down' – code for 'putting them to bed for a sleep'. You could experiment for yourself as to when the best time for a change is, or you could save time and trouble by accepting that all mothers know best.

To change him, find a flat surface, such as on the carpet or on a worktop. If you're working up high, keep one hand on his belly, otherwise he'll roll or crawl off towards danger and leave you to take the blame.

Step 1. Place him on his back, with your replacement nappy unfurled underneath him so that if he decides to backfire everywhere it's not going all over your cream shagpile. (A similar damage-limitation tip is to place a tissue over his front tail, otherwise he may unleash his party piece: pissing in your eye.) Make sure the end with the sticky tabs is under his back.

Step 2. Undo the soiled nappy, retch at the pungent horror, then use the clean sections of the nappy to wipe away any mess round his parts. Grab both his ankles with one hand, raise his backside to the roof and remove the nappy. Fold securely and place out of his reach, to be disposed of later.

Step 3. Now, using either cotton wool and water or baby wipes, clean what mess remains, taking care to get into any creases. If you use wipes, check for any rashes and apply a nappy-rash cream if required. If left to irritate your baby, the rash will wake him in the middle of the night, and then he'll wake you by screaming at the top of his voice. If that happens, you'll wish you'd paid attention to this advice.

Remember to only ever wipe the baby from front to back, especially if he's a girl, otherwise you risk spreading the bacteria that can cause urinary tract infections, and nobody wants that.

Step 4. Having patted him dry, lower him onto that clean nappy, pull the front section through his legs and the back bit to the front at the sides with the sticky tabs. Dispose of the dirty nappy in a special nappy bag or bin as quickly as humanly possible.

Step 5. Finally, wash your hands and wait a full five minutes until he needs changing again.

How To ...
Skim A Stone Across Water

This is the one trick guaranteed to impress small children and women, but only if your skim bounces at least half a dozen times. Anything less is a waste of everyone's time.

The good news is that a team of French boffins investigated stone-skimming and discovered that it all comes down to the kinematic viscosity of the water, which is pretty much what we all suspected. However, they also found out that $\frac{1}{2}MV_x^2[N] - \frac{1}{2}MV_x^2[0] = -N\mu Mgl$, which was quite a shock, certainly to me. Anyway, in layman's terms, it seems your chances of a double-figure skim are increased significantly by following several simple rules ...

Rule 1. The water should be as still as possible, for obvious reasons, while the stone should be flat and circular to encourage more bounce.

Rule 2. A common misconception in this game is that to muster enough power for a double-figure spin, you'll need to lob the stone in as fast as physically possible. Speed of entry into the water does count, but only when it's combined with spin. This stabilizes the stone through the water and maximizes the number of bounces you'll achieve.

On releasing the stone, spin it in a clockwise direction, or anticlockwise if you're left handed.

Rule 3. The perfect angle of entry is bang on 20 degrees. Anything less and it will lose much of its energy dragging through the water, anything over 45 degrees and it won't bounce, just sink. Like a stone.

Rule 4. You'll need to spin the bugger more than 14 times per second and skim faster than 12 m^{s-1} to come close to the current world record of 39 bounces (Toxteth O'Grady, USA). M^{s-1}? Nope, no idea either. Just concentrate on spinning the stone with your index finger as you release it. Flick it in a clockwise direction as marked (if your're right-handed) to increase its speed of rotation. The greater the flick, the greater the rotation and sure enough, the greater the skim.

How To...
Fight A Raging Fire*

First, a timely caveat. Everyone knows Big Fires should be avoided at all costs. At the first sign of a proper big blaze you should leg it outside and call the firefighters (tel: 999). However, a small blaze such as the ever popular Chip-Pan Fire can be extinguished with a minimum of fuss ...

Step 1. Under no circumstances attempt to move the pan: that oil is both boiling and burning and liable to cause you great pain.

Step 2. Instead, if you can safely reach the controls without leaning over the pan, turn the cooker off. (If you can't, accept defeat and call the fire service.)

Step 3. Resist the urge to throw water over the flames; oil and water don't mix and you'll create a fireball accompanied by a small explosion.

Step 4. Drape a fire blanket carefully over the pan.

Step 5. No, I've no idea what a fire blanket is or where you'd find one either, so run a tea towel (or cloth) under a tap, wring it out fully and cover the pan with that instead.

Step 6. The flames should die down. Leave the pan to cool completely, make yourself a sandwich for tea and learn these fire prevention tips off by heart:

- I must never fill my pan more than one-third full.
- I must dry all food before introducing it to hot oil – any water may make the oil explode.
- I should take smoking oil as a warning sign that it's too hot. I will turn it off and let it cool.
- I should never ever leave a chip pan unattended, not even to tell the crone at the door where to stick her lucky pegs.
- I will always be asleep between 10 p.m. and 4 a.m., aware that most house fire incidents happen between those hours, mainly when drunken morons decide they want chips.

Warning: the fire services advise against you fighting a fire, unless it's a small one that can be brought under control by an untrained civilian. Only approach fires with extreme caution. And consider yourself warned.

How To...
Buy A Suit That Actually Looks Good On You

If you're the type of man who enjoys paying a small fortune to have his inner thighs felt up by a ferrety old man, this entry is not for you. Take your bespoke three-piece and flounce on to the next entry.

If you're the type of man who needs a decent suit but doesn't want to have to sell both kidneys on eBay to fund it, the following basic rules should hold you in good stead ...

The head

The easiest but most important rule of all: make your own mind up. By all means consider the opinions of your yapping female companion who prefers you in lilac, and the smarmy sales assistant who works on commission. The final decision, however, must always be yours. If it doesn't look and feel right to you, you've just wasted your money.

The jacket – plain or striped fabric?

Pinstripes come in thousands of combinations and suit City bankers and estate agents, so let's discard that option straight away. If in doubt, choose a plain fabric. It's generally more versatile and goes about its business with quiet, understated efficiency. Check suits are another option, if you don't mind dressing like a clown.

Double- or single-breasted?

This is a matter of taste. Double-breasted are less common, somewhat retro, and most likely to be found on the male captain of the local golf club. He knows it makes him look distinguished as he escorts the ladies and other undesirables from the premises. Single-breasted is the safer option.

Single-breasted   Double-breasted

Arm holes

It's worth paying a little extra for a suit with two arm holes, and the basic rule is that they should be tight but comfortable. Hold both arms up over your head – if the material's too tight, the jacket will ride up and show off the back of your shirt, which is not good.

Cuffs

A good test to ensure correct cuff-length is to let your arms hang loose and then curl up your hands. If the jacket cuffs touch the middle of each palm, the length's about right. The amount of shirt showing beneath the cuff is down to the individual. A centimetre and a bit is considered about right, unless you happen to be wearing spanking-new cufflinks you want to show off, in which case just under 4 cm is more like it.

Length of jacket

This varies depending on your shape, but as a general guide, a regular suit jacket should be about level with the top of your buttocks.

Vents

A finishing touch to be found at the rear of the jacket. Vents help slim the upper body and come in three options: a single vent in the centre, one either side, or none at all.

No vents Suits the thin man by allowing the jacket to naturally hang straight at the sides and widen his scrawny profile.

Single vent The most popular option, designed for the average-build man carrying a little baggage around the midriff. The vent encourages the jacket to stretch and sit more comfortably, reducing unsightly lumps and bumps. The vent also makes the bottom of the jacket flair slightly on either side, giving the impression you're fairly well defined in the chest area.

Twin vents Best for chunky monkeys. They ensure the suit sits more comfortably, giving the impression of a slimmer stomach and a more defined chest, and could well save you from death by suffocation.

Lapels

You can judge a man by his lapel.

Medium lapel The safety-first default setting, for the man who doesn't want to make any bold statements.

Thin lapel Works best on trim men, particularly trim men who want to display a more flamboyant, individual streak.

Wide lapel This man has a slightly retro, wild-at-heart streak. It's probably a cry for help and shouldn't ever be worn to a job interview.

The length of the lapel can also be used to lengthen or shorten your upper body. A long, thin lapel (teamed with one or two front buttons on the jacket and plain, flat-fronted trousers) will lengthen the upper body – good news for stocky men with short upper bodies (squaddies, rugby players and bouncers), and men with large upper bodies who want to appear a little slimmer.

Trousers

Obviously it's beneficial if they're cut from the same cloth as the jacket, and when you stand bolt upright the trouser legs should rest on the tops of your shoes and crease 5 or 6 centimetres higher. That's officially a snug fit.

Crotch

As a general rule, you need enough room to put your hands in your pockets without discomfort. If you can play pocket billiards without disrupting the fabric, they're too big. If your old chap is visible beneath the fabric every time you sit down, you need a more generous cut.

Pleats and turn-ups

Both very popular in the 1980s, therefore to be avoided at

all costs. And here's a free tip for the vertically challenged: non-pleated, plain-fronted, straight-legged slacks without turn-ups will create the appearance of longer, thinner legs. Obviously, for gangling chaps wishing to look a little more compact the opposite applies, and pleats and turn-ups are sadly back in.

How To ...
Start A Frozen Car In Winter Weather

If your car has frozen overnight it almost certainly won't start, which means you won't be able to get in to work today and can spend your day learning How To ... Become A Multi-Millionaire In Five Working Days (Or Your Money Back) – see page 234.

If you're still reading, you clearly have no choice but to make it into work today for some important presentation or other, or to deliver a package to someone several miles away, or some other such scenario. So, for those who need to start a car in freezing conditions, here's what to do ...

Plan ahead

A big freeze will sap the car battery's power, rendering it completely useless. If the weather man predicts a cold snap overnight (let's say -10 °C (14 °F)), whip out your car's battery the night before, having first consulted your car manual on how that can be done most safely. Bring the battery indoors and wrap a blanket around it to show that you really care. If you're really serious about getting to work every day in Arctic conditions, it would also help if you changed to a lightweight winter oil, rather than a heavier oil which can hinder engine efficiency.

Damage limitation

If you ignore all of the above and wake to find your car has frozen, the quickest way to defrost it is by attaching a hose to the exhaust of a working car and feeding the other end under the engine of your vehicle. Once warmed back to life, the engine should be easier to start. Even so, make sure the heater, radio, all the lights and anything else that will sap the battery's energy are all switched off before you turn the ignition key.

Turning tricks

Turn and hold the key for five to ten seconds, but if it's an older car (and therefore a non-fuel-injected model), you'll need to give it just a little gas – a few pumps will suffice, but don't overdo things. If it's fuel-injected, the clever computer chip running the injectors will find for you an optimum petrol flow to start the engine.

If it doesn't start, let the car rest for a couple of minutes before trying again – over-grinding the starter will cause mechanical damage that costs money to repair.

Pulling off

Finally, having followed all of the above, your engine has started. Do not pull straight off and floor it, wheel-spinning away in a fug of smoke. Allow the engine to tick over for a couple of minutes until it's properly warmed up and the oil has moved through the engine. Cold oil coursing through the car can bugger up your engine badly and increase your blood pressure. After a couple of minutes, put the car in gear and be about your business.

How To...
Open Champagne
(The Sophisticated, Unflustered Way)

If you've paid good money for posh booze, the least you can do is open it properly and give the impression you drink this stuff all the time – although not to the point of it being a problem or anything.

However, before you even think about opening the champagne, make certain it's been in an ice bucket long enough to chill properly – it needs to be 7°C (45°F), according to the experts. Cool champagne tastes all wrong, warm champagne tastes even worse and is far more likely to foam and spill when you open the bottle, making you look like a fat-fingered oaf. Once chilled, you're ready to open and pour...

Step 1. Take a nice, crisp white cloth and dry off the bottle to allow you to get a better grip on it. Remove the foil from the top of the bottle, then loosen and remove the wire cage surrounding the cork. With the bottle upright, drape the cloth over the top – she'll think this looks professional; no need to mention it's there to catch the cork should it accidentally shoot out and smack her in the eye. With the cage removed, the pressure inside the bottle can sometimes force the cork out on its own and send it across the room at speeds of up to 180 mph. It's probably best to keep your thumb on the cork throughout.

Step 2. Lower the bottle so it's at a 45-degree angle, with the towel now draped over the neck of the bottle and concealing it from view. Hold the neck of the bottle in one hand, with your thumb still firmly atop the cork. With your other hand, grip and very gently twist the bottle, *never the cork*. Keep turning slowly until you hear a gentle 'pop' – only impatient amateurs, racing drivers and smug City bankers get the loud popping sound, which comes when the bubble-inducing carbon dioxide escapes from the bottle, followed by a hearty spurt of your expensive booze. Whip off the cloth, give the lady a knowing look, and prepare to pour. Having dedicated so much time and effort to uncorking the bugger, you'll need a suitable receptacle. Paper cups, chipped mugs and those oversized northern beer tankards with windows are unsuitable and will undermine your work thus far. If this woman (or man, could be a man) means anything to you, invest in two tasteful champagne flutes.

Step 3. Unlike foaming ale, champagne doesn't require a frothy head – merely a few classy bubbles. The secret is to angle the flute and pour in just a little champagne – just over a centimetre or so should do for now. Wait a few seconds for the bubbles to disappear, then pour again until two-thirds of the glass is full. Drink holding the stem of the glass so as not to warm the champagne, chill the bottle in between pouring, and try not to belch.

Size matters

Champagne bottles come in more than one size:

Split or Piccolo (187.5 ml or 200 ml) – A quarter bottle, one for the ladies to suck through a straw

Demi (375 ml) – A cheeky half-bottle

Imperial (750 ml) – A bog-standard bottle

Magnum (1.5 l) – 2 bottles in one

Jeroboam (3 l) – 4 bottles

Rehoboam (4.5 l) – 6 bottles

Methuselah (6 l) – 8 bottles

Salmanazar (9 l) – Just the 12

Balthazar (12 l) – 16 bottles

Nebuchadnezzar (15 l) – 20 bottles

Melchior (18 l) – 24 bottles

Solomon (25 l) – 33.3 bottles

Primat (27 l) – 36 bottles

Melchizedek (30 l) – 40 bottles, and you couldn't lift this fucker, let alone open and drink it.

How To ...
Be The Perfect Gentleman

The good news for all men is that you no longer need to be a braying toff to be a gentleman, unlike in the old days when it was all based on bloodlines, bank accounts and interbreeding. These days, according to the *Oxford English Dictionary*, a gent is defined as nothing more than 'a courteous or honourable man'.

He doesn't have to be from posh stock and, luckily, there are so many unruly scrotes in society these days that even the occasional act of courtesy – particularly when directed towards a woman – will elevate you instantly above the rabble.

Consider the following ten skills as mere pointers towards a more gentlemanly existence. They are merely the basics; the mark of a true gent is that he's always keen to learn more. But space on the page is tight and, well, they're a start ...

Rule 1. A true gent goes about his business with the minimum of fuss and drama. Nothing should surprise him or cause him to show dismay in public; not a run of ill-fortune on the nags, nor the loss of his entire family in a bizarre yachting accident. Life's many tribulations cannot shake him from his stride.

Rule 2. A true gent never swears. His vocabulary should be sufficiently mature for him not to have to resort to the language of the gutter. Even when the talk around him is turning fruity, he never lowers himself to such levels. However, if he does have to say 'fuck' or 'bugger' for any reason, he'll first check over both shoulders to make sure no ladies are within earshot.

Rule 3. Only a vulgar man will be seen spitting on the floor. If he has to gob he should cough it up into a handkerchief – without making that big, guttural, phlegmy sound – and dispose of it later. Similarly, a man should never be seen rummaging a finger up his nostril, let alone waving his dirty catch around for all to see. Use a handkerchief, and don't give the contents more than a cursory glance.

Rule 4. A gentleman must walk like a gentleman: upright with his head held high. Never shuffle along dragging your knuckles and feet, nor swagger like a dandy. Aim for something in between and you should be safe.

Rule 5. A true gent knows how to conduct himself around women. He's punctual and polite. He stands when she enters the room, offers her his seat and helps her with her coat or the door. He maintains eye contact, laughs politely at her jokes, and treats her as an equal, even when buying her drinks all night or carrying a box that she claims is too heavy for her skinny frame. She may just be being bone-idle, but a gent would know better than to bandy around accusations.

Rule 6. A gent also knows how to behave in mixed company at the dinner table. The list of gourmet rules is too lengthy to cover here, suffice to say that elbows should be kept off the table, talking with a full trap is frowned upon, and soup should be sipped not slurped. Also, if a gent discovers a hair in his food while dining, he does the gentlemanly thing and places it beneath the edge of his plate with the minimum of fuss, rather than accusing the chef of sticking his privates in the soufflé again.

Rule 7. A gentleman never ever laughs at the misfortunes of others, unless he happens to see three pensioners careering haphazardly down a hill in a bath on TV. Then he can laugh quite literally like a drain to confirm his well-rounded sense of humour.

Rule 8. A gentleman never carries a watch, partly because he'd never frequent the rough parts of town where there were no public clocks, but mainly because he could always ask his butler if he needed to know the hour. You can consider this one optional.

Rule 9. A gentleman never invites a woman to pull his finger. This one's *not* optional.

Rule 10. And a gentleman is never unconsciously rude or disagreeable. When he is rude or disagreeable, it's because he means to be – and on these occasions he's allowed to say 'fuck' and 'bugger' all he likes.

How To ...
Rugby-Tackle A Thief

Get this right and there's probably a token reward on offer from the shopkeeper for putting your life on the line. If the thief's making it easy for you, he'll be the one in the black-and-white sweater carrying the bag marked 'SWAG'. You'll need to bring the brute down and sit on him until Plod finally turns up, but how you stop him depends on which direction you're tackling him from ...

Tackle from the front

If the thief's been stupid enough to scarper towards you with his head held high and his chest exposed, your job's much easier. You'll want to wind him by nailing him in the stomach with your shoulder, as hard as you can. So, taking the rugby-tackle approach, as your shoulder makes contact with his gut, drive through with your legs to maximize the impact and sit on him while he struggles to recover. If his head is down and his chest less exposed, aim to stick your shoulder between his hip and abdomen, grab round the backs of his legs and lift with a straight back to dump him on his arse. Or you could just opt for the safer option by allowing him to run past you before tackling him from the back.

Tackle from the back

The safest option of all. Approaching from the rear, focus on the back of the thief's thighs and get as close to him as possible. When in range, make contact with your shoulder on his thigh and position your head to one side of his leg. Straighten your back and wrap both arms around him. The combined momentum should see you slide down his legs and bring him to the floor, provided you manage to hang on for dear life.

Important disclaimer: Many thieves can be quite bad-tempered if you bother them while they're working. Attempt this trick at your own discretion – and don't come crying to us if the thief stoves your head in.

How To ...
Blow A Smoke Ring

Society may look down its nose at cigarette smokers these days, but the man who can fire smoke rings from his gob while puffing on a cigar remains the first name on any guest list. And rightly so: this chap's a suave entertainer who tweaks the nose of cancer just to keep you amused ...

Your weapon of choice

If you want to be that man, you'll need a fat cigar. Although smoke rings can be achieved using a standard cigarette, it'll make you look like a bus-station ratboy. Pipes produce enough smoke for a good ring, but they're reserved for weird uncles and social inadequates. So a good Cuban cigar works best.

The bog-standard basic

Suck up a generous mouthful of smoke, but don't inhale or the trick will fall flat on its arse. You'll need to purse your lips as if you're about to say the letter 'O'. The size of that 'O' determines the size of the smoke ring – start small and build up. As you tighten your throat muscles, the underside of your tongue needs to flick the smoke out as a small puff of air – tongue control is everything here and you'll cough and splutter before you've mastered the art.

Getting the volume of smoke right is key – too little smoke and people will think you've merely coughed; too much smoke and they'll move away to someone less carcinogenic.

Trick puffs

With practice comes the ability to entertain entire dinner parties with your pollution. You've learnt that the size of the 'O' determines the size of the ring, and trial and error will teach you how the duration and velocity of the exhalation controls the speed, while flexing your throat muscles allows you to shoot off rapid-fire rings.

Larger rings move more slowly through the air, which allows you the time to pull off the easiest piece of smoke-ring showmanship. Using the bog-standard basic technique, send a large ring out into the air, then fire a smaller, faster-moving ring through its centre. Get it right and you'll prove once and for all that smoking is actually both big *and* clever.

How To ...
Pull Off The Heimlich Manoeuvre

If there's one thing guaranteed to ruin a pleasant meal out amongst lively company, it's noticing that one of your fellow diners is choking to death on their starter. The telltale signs are that they've turned a worrying shade of blue and started grasping their throat and gasping for air. These symptoms suggest that their windpipe has become blocked, and without assistance they'll surely die. Needn't panic though, for the trusty Heimlich Manoeuvre should save them.

First, encourage the victim to cough – that in itself could be enough to dislodge the object. If they can't cough, slap them on the back sharply five times, then check their mouth to see if the object has dislodged. If not, have someone call an ambulance (that bit is important) as you perform the Heimlich ...

Step 1. Wrap your arms around the ailing person's waist. Now, make a fist and place the thumb-side of it against the choker's upper abdomen, i.e. below the ribcage and above the navel. Tell your fellow diners not to panic, that you know what you're doing, you've done this sort of thing before, and so on and so forth. Keeping everyone calm is very important.

Step 2. Next, grasp your fist with your spare hand and press into their upper abdomen with a quick upward thrust. Squeezing the ribcage with your arms could inflict damage, so confine the force of the thrust to your hands.

Step 3. If you're lucky, there will be no Step 3: whatever was blocking the windpipe should at this point pop back out of their mouth. If it does, don't eat it. If it doesn't, repeat Step 2 until the object's expelled. Suggest to the victim that if they doubt the object has been completely removed they should proceed directly to a doctor, then let the waiter know that you have no intention of paying the bill.

The good doctor

Since its introduction in 1974, Dr Henry J. Heimlich's trusty manoeuvre has saved more than 50,000 people, including the likes of celebrity chokers Ronald Reagan, Liz Taylor and Princess Leia, or at least the woman who played her. Also, it can and has been used to save numerous pets who've been choking on nuts and dog biscuits and the like. Opinions as to its effectiveness vary across the world – it's banned in several countries, including Australia, due to the risk of injury even when performed correctly – but the Heimlich is generally considered to be the safest way of saving a choking victim.

How To ...
Survive In Prison

Very much a worst-case scenario, this, but you never know. Let's say, for the sake of argument, you're facing a five-year stretch for something you may or may not have done. You claim it was a fit-up, but then your sort always do.

Now we could offer the usual half-baked advice – avoid getting into debt to Mr Big, pack a good supply of soap on a rope, never lend a crack addict your Mars bar – and it would all be very valid. But for the novice lag checking into Big House for the first time, unless you know your apple from your salmon, you could end up playing patsy.

A is for ...
Apple Basic prison rhyming slang: apple core = score = 20, as in years, or £20.

B is for ...
Bang up Time spent locked up in a 3-foot-by-1-foot cell, with only a 6-foot-7-inch serial killer for company.

Baron, the A feared and influential inmate who's happy to lend or sell goods – generally snout and drugs – only at an unreasonably high, non-negotiable rate of interest. Pay up or expect a bed-leg to the head.

Bed-leg A weapon made from a section of steel pipe used

to separate prison bunk beds, often slipped inside a sock. Likely to smart on contact.

Bunnies Ecstacy, the drug. So called as it makes an inmate go up and down like a psychotic rabbit.

Burn Tobacco. Very popular on the inside.

C is for ...
Chicken Lag code word for cannabis. They think the Screws haven't cottoned on to this, but they have.

Chip net The safety net strung between landings and designed to catch any falling lag.

D is for ...
Daddy, the Respected for the length of time he's spent in Big House, this man can be a valuable source of advice. Approach with caution, asking yourself why he's been in so long and where those funny lines down his face came from.

Diesel Prison tea, generally served on the strong side. Decaf diesel is not an option.

Duff Pudding. Could be tiramisu or an individual pear tartlet, although it's far more likely to look like an individual splat of something brown with a sorry dribble of powdered Bird's.

G is for ...
Ghosting The act of being transferred to another prison, at short notice, without warning and quite possibly by the

scruff of your neck. All ghosting is carried out by the Mufti Squad. Why Mufti? No idea. I asked, they couldn't say.

Gofer A weak individual manipulated by other inmates: 'Gofer this, gofer that.' Can often be heard weeping in the toilet and also answers to the names Joe and Joey. Ironically, some gofers *are* called Joe.

J is for ...
Jam-roll Not a pastry-based pudding, but a rhyming slang reference to parole.

Jimmy or *Jimmy Boyle* More slang, this time referring to tin foil, used by crackheads to smoke their drugs. Just say no, kids.

K is for ...
Kangas Kanga = Kangaroo = Screw, the prison officers, who may also be known as Scoobys – Scoobydoo – etc.

L is for ...
L-plates If you're saddled with these, you're in for a life sentence and must have committed a most heinous crime. By the time you leave, expect to have learnt far more prison lingo than is listed here.

Line In order to pass an item after lock-up, prisoners make a line and move it on. It's probably a map of a new tunnel.

M is for ...
Midnight More slang, this time: Midnight mass = grass. An unpopular career move in Big House.

N is for ...
Numpty A psychiatrically disturbed inmate.

O is for ...
Old man The Prison Governor, the man in charge. The name's misleading, for he won't have white hair or need a chairlift to navigate the stairs. Not suggesting anything untoward would happen otherwise, but it's wise to keep on the right side of him.

P is for ...
Patsy This unfortunate chap takes the blame for others. He's a fall guy, done up like a kippah.

Peter thief Unpopular character who steals from other prisoners' cells. He robs Peter to pay Paul and can expect a bed-leg to the head from Mad Maurice McMad for his trouble.

Pie and liquor Prison slang: the Vicar. Feel free to confess your many sins, for what you tell him should – in theory – go no further.

R is for ...
Runners In return for not being beaten to a pulp in the toilets, these men are happy to fetch and carry for more powerful inmates. Also known as wingers.

S is for ...
Salmon More slang, this time it's short for salmon and trout – snout, as in cigarettes.

Shit and a shave If you're only in for a shit and a shave, you have a short sentence and your jam roll is imminent. May also be referred to as a *shit and a shower*.

Spin If your cell is searched by the Screws, you've had a 'pad spin'. If they find what they're looking for, a visit to the Old Man may follow.

Stiff A smuggled note, often moved along the line and featuring a map of Big House basement.

T is for ...
Tram lines A nasty double-line scar caused by a prison-made weapon – a melted-down toothbrush head with two disposable razor blades stuck in the end. It hurts, but the ingenuity can only be admired.

W is for ...
Wet-up Should you irk a fellow inmate, he may opt to throw boiling water and sugar in your face. The sugar makes the water stick, which tends to sting. Also known as jug-up, and every bit as painful.

X, Y & Z is for ...
... Nothing. Big House is no place for smart-arses.

How To...
Catch A Fish With A Piece Of String

In theory, with enough training from bearded men who survive in the wilderness and live off the land, you could easily make a fishing line from numerous plant and inner bark fibres, just as your ancestors did. Attach a bone sharpened into a dangerous point and you'd have yourself a make-do hook with which you could snare fish all day long. Alas, there's no room on this page for all that, so let's agree that you're sat by a river feeling a little bit peckish, armed with nothing more than a line of string and a dash of cunning.

There are around fifty species of freshwater fish in British rivers, many of which taste good with chips and mayonnaise. One of the tastiest, the trout, loiters lazily in well-oxygenated freshwater rivers, and can be caught using the following technique.

Step 1. Hang around close to the river bank, in a position where you can observe what's going on beneath the water. Sunglasses with polarized lenses, which cut the surface glare, make it easier to spot a fish. Did you pack your sunglasses? No, ah. Then ignore that bit and concentrate on keeping low to reduce your profile against the sky – if the fish spots you he's guaranteed to scarper. You'll need to draw him towards you with tasty bait – earthworms and flies remain popular among fish. Take your bait and insert a line of fine thread through its body, using the penknife we know you will have packed. Then run the line through a small thorn that will act as a make-do hook, and tie it all securely in place with a good-sized knot at the end. Drop the line into the water and wait, making sure your shadow doesn't fall across the water and spook the fish.

Step 2. And wait.

Step 3. And be prepared to wait some more – stealth and patience are key here.

Finally, when a hungry fish takes the bait, the thorn should lodge in its throat or mouth. As he panics and you feel your line tighten, pull him on to the bank.

An alternative approach
If your line is particularly fibrous, you could hunt eel rather than trout. Back in the olden days, fishermen would attach a gaggle of worms to the end of a line and wait for the eel to take the bait. Those fine fibres on the line would attach very easily to the eel's teeth, and no amount of wriggling would save him from the fisherman's clutches.

Another alternative
If you only have a length of thread or fine string and no bait, you could always tie it into a simple slipknot noose, drop it into the water and wait for the fish to float towards you. Without bait, this should take even longer than normal and you may fall asleep before you even sniff a catch. But if a fish is unlucky enough to float within range,

gently manoeuvre the noose onto its tail or around the gills, tighten in a flash and haul it out onto the river bank. This method is apparently also good for snaring small birds, but they don't taste quite as nice.

Tickling trout

Legend has it that if you wait long enough in a river a trout will present itself and allow you to tickle its belly. Then, after a couple of minutes, the tickling will send the trout into a blissful doze, at which point you lift him straight out the river and into a deep-fat fryer. Sadly, the truth is less impressive. To catch trout by hand, you'll need to skulk about on the bank of a shallow, fast-flowing river or stream.* Feel gently around the stones and rocks, where trout like to loiter, until you touch something slimy – this should be the fish you've been looking for. Act fast to grip firmly around the underbelly and whip the fish out onto the bank before he can dart off downstream. Once he's on dry land, you can tickle him all you want.

*This assumes you've paid for a legitimate permit to fish on the waters in question. It's illegal, otherwise.

How To ...
Save A Drowning Person

You'll need to think fast here, although not so fast that you don't first consider the dangers involved to you, the would-be hero. Your natural instinct may be to dive head-first into the swim and drag the thrashing drowner to safety, but you'd be a tad premature and endangering your own life ...

Warning: Only ever enter the water as a last resort

If there's a stick or pole to hand, hold it out and suggest the swimmer (well, drowner) hangs on as you haul him back to safety. If someone's thoughtfully hung a life ring on the end of a rope nearby, lob that instead and haul him back to dry land. Either way, make sure you're secure on the sidelines as you pull, so as not to get yanked in yourself. Finally, if there happens to be a boat to hand, row out to the victim before employing the stick or ring methods.

If this stretch of water is lacking long sticks, floating rings and useful boats, the only option is to enter the water – **But Only If You're A Trained Lifeguard**. If you're not, you've officially done all you can for this person and should now call for assistance from the emergency services (tel: 999 or 112) and wait. Unless you're trained, you should under no circumstances enter the water, even if the drowning person is a member of your family or a close friend who owes you money.

The danger is that in their blind panic, drowning people often drag their rescuer under the water as they struggle, very selfishly putting two lives at risk. A trained lifeguard would know that it's vital to talk to the victim as he approaches and to tell him he's about to help him back to shore. That would calm him down and allow the rescuer to hook his arm over the victim's chest from behind. He could then tell him to relax and float on his back to make things easier, as he used his free arm to sidestroke them both back to safety.

If the victim does drag this trained hero down, he'd know to swim down further under the water, aware that the victim will fight to return to the surface and thus set him free. Once back on shore, the expert would know to check the victim's airway, breathing and circulation, and how to administer the kiss of life, if required (which he may have learnt on pages 142–4). He'd also know to treat them with extreme care throughout so as not to exacerbate any injuries already sustained.

That's what he'd do. You, of course, are not trained so should stand helplessly on the river bank and watch as the victim disappears under the water.

Warning: this is based on relatively still waters rather than any stretch with dangerous undercurrents. Diving into the water is a risky business and you could lose your life. Man Skills *cannot recommend it, although a good lawyer will notice that we have already repeatedly advised against entering the water if you don't know what you're doing.*

How To ...
Toss A Caber

Cabers have been thrown about by hairy brutes for centuries, often in warfare, when large logs were tossed into enemy battlements, or as a practical solution to logistical problems – logs were often chucked across rivers as makeshift bridges. Only in more recent times have cabers been tossed by men in skirts for the sheer unadulterated buzz of it all.

Measure up

The professionals typically toss a 6-metre-long caber weighing between 35 to 60 kilograms – which is almost certainly out of your league. Unless you want to do yourself an injury, use a scaled-down version – which is shorter and lighter, and therefore easier to control. First though, consider the following ...

Distance is irrelevant

Caber tossing is marked on technique and landing. To score high you'll need the caber to turn 180 degrees (end over end) in the air, land on what started out as the top end and fall directly away from you at what the professionals call the 12 o'clock position. In competition, 12:00 rules, but 11:00 scores higher than 9:00, just as 1:00 is better than 3:00. If the caber lands on its end and falls back towards you, run for cover and expect to be marked down accordingly – forward falls always score higher than those dropping backwards. But we're getting ahead of ourselves here, because first you'll need to master the technique.

The technique

Assume the correct manly posture: heels together, toes out, the narrow end of the caber lying flat on the ground between your feet and facing away from you, mild fear etched across your face. The far end of the caber will be lifted off the floor and walked up towards you and into an upright position, so that it's now staring you straight in the face. At this point, it's probably too late to back out.

Step 1. Seasoned professionals will have coated their hands in tacky, a resin-and-turpentine mix that feels like treacle and keeps their mitts securely on the caber. Without tacky, your fingers will almost certainly be driven apart and the caber will fall on your foot.

Step 2. So, lock your gloopy fingers together, bend at the knees and grip the caber. Get as much of your palms as possible around its base, dig both hands in firmly and stand up. Do it slowly and use your leg muscles rather than your arms to lift. The caber should come up easily enough, but then it gets tricky.

Step 3. The caber is now vertical and resting against your stronger shoulder, but half the battle is steadying the thing. You can expect to spend several minutes staggering around like a drunkard before you have it under full control, and only then are you finally ready to launch it.

Step 4. The technique can vary. Some people take a long run up, others just a few steps – do whatever feels most comfortable to you. With either approach, as you move forward, try to run the final few steps to gain momentum. As you approach the line, push the caber forward with your shoulder until it reaches a suitable launching angle (at least 45 degrees, at most 75), then drive your hands and arms forwards and upwards to create as much thrust as possible.

Now, stand back and watch it arc off into the distance, or run for cover and scream like a child as it drops back towards your head.

Tossers beware!

To attempt this skill, seasoned tossers warn that you'll need to be in 'good physical shape', otherwise you're likely to pull or twang something painful. Consult a gym instructor for a definition of 'good physical shape', and mention to him that you'll need to work on your leg strength as that's where much of your tossing power will come from.

A load of old toss

For all you etymology fans out there, you might like to know that the word 'caber' comes from the early-sixteenth-century Scots Gaelic word *cabar*, meaning 'pole'. Or you might not. But it's too late now.

How To ...
Deliver A Baby In An Emergency

First things first, a legal warning to consider before attempting this one: it's unlawful for anyone other than a registered midwife or doctor to plan to deliver a baby for other people. If you attempt to set up a lucrative business based on what you learn from this entry, you should expect a knock on the door from Plod followed by a large fine or a stretch inside.

This entry is for Times of Emergency Only, and you'll probably never have to call upon the wisdom it imparts. If you do, fret not, for your job can be summarized as a simple Catch and Dry operation. Hospital births have become a matter of custom rather than a matter of need only in the last 100 years or so. Before then, women were dropping newborns in fields, cowsheds and ditches full of dung with little trouble. The point being laboured here is that it's a natural event, not something to fear.

So, the method

There's no time to get the expectant mother to hospital, so you'll have to birth him (could be a her, but we're saying him) yourself.

Step 1. Luckily, babies do much of the work themselves, so you just need to be on hand to coax, cajole and calm mother down when she gets flustered. Keep telling her everything will be fine, she's in safe hands, you've read about it in that book she bought you for Christmas. Then call your midwife, then an ambulance – in that order.

Step 2. Make sure she's in a comfortable position on her hands and knees, close to the floor and forward-leaning so that the baby can traverse the pelvis in a natural way. Despite what you've seen on *Casualty*, she shouldn't be on her back on a bed. That's for the benefit of the doctor so he can see more clearly – plus the sight of a woman giving birth with her backside in the air is not so TV-friendly.

Don't encourage her to push. Women are generally very adept at delivering babies and their bodies will tell them when and how to breathe. Barking instructions like some jumped up sergeant major may make you feel better about your minimal contribution, but it's helping nobody.

Step 3. Check to see if the baby's head is visible. If not, continue as you were, encouraging, glancing occasionally at your watch and wondering what's taking that midwife so long.

If his head is visible, inform the mother, wait for the shoulders to emerge and then support the head in your hands and guide him gently towards the floor. Don't yank him out, you impatient oaf, he'll come out soon enough.

Step 4. The minute babies hit cold air, 99 per cent of them take a deep breath and begin to wail.

If they don't begin breathing, they'll need mild resuscitation, which sounds more dramatic than it is.

Simply take a towel and gently dry him off, working from the head down, taking special care around the soft spot on the top of the head (the fontanelle). Towelling warms and stimulates the baby, at which point he'll take a breath in and open his lungs loudly in your ear.

Step 5. More perceptive men may notice that the baby is still attached to the mother by the umbilical cord. This can remain attached safely for several weeks if need be, so there's no rush to cut it, particularly as you don't know what you're doing. Leave it for the midwife, because she does.

Step 6. Finally, wrap the baby in a dry towel and pass him to his mother, who should by now be sweaty, glowing and teary-eyed. Shrug it off like it was no problem, then toast the new lad with a stiff drink.

How To ...
Hold A Baby Properly

By properly, we mean without dropping it on its delicate little head or allowing its neck to loll painfully to the side. The good news is that babies come with a clever built-in alarm that can gauge when you're holding them just right. The bad news is that until you get it right that alarm will scream until your ears drip blood.

The fact of the matter is that there's no right or wrong way to hold a baby, and no expert technique that only mothers know. It's simply trial and error, shuffling the baby round until he's comfortable – at which point he'll stop bawling and begin dribbling on your shirt. That said, to avoid being patronized by any woman observing your ham-fisted attempts, memorize this idiot-proof technique.

With the baby in a lying position, scoop him up and hold his front against your chest, with his head turned to one side. Use one hand and forearm to support his bottom and take the weight, and the other to fully support his back, neck and head.

The single undisputable law of Baby Holding is that you have to fully support his body, particularly the head and neck, because he doesn't yet have the strength or control to do it himself.

The key to any good hold is that you both need to be comfortable, but his comfort is far more important than yours and he's likely to scream until he vomits if you don't get it right.

As this man recognizes, the most important thing is to provide support to the baby's head.

How To ...
Pass Yourself Off As Some Kind Of Wine Buff

By 'wine buff' we mean the type of man who can order a half-decent bottle in a restaurant without coming across as a pompous old blowhard. Whether it's a first date, an important lunch with people in suits or an attempt to win over suspicious in-laws whom you suspect might think you're hapless, stick to these ten basic rules and you won't go wrong. Or, at least, not too far wrong ...

Basic Rules

1. Never ask the wine waiter to recommend a wine. How do you know for sure that he knows what he's talking about? And if he works on commission, what's to stop him steering you towards a more expensive bottle? Do it yourself.

2. Don't let him pressure you into choosing. If you feel rushed in any way, simply make eye contact, project confidence and say, 'Thank you, we'll decide shortly.' Never be pushed into choosing a wine you're unsure of or anything out of your price range.

3. Look for grape varieties and countries. Wily wine producers stick different labels on restaurant wine so you don't notice that you're ordering the same bottle you can get for £3.99 in a supermarket. Remember which grape varieties and countries you normally like, rather than the pretty sticker on the front, so that you recognize the name of a favoured tipple when you spot it on a restaurant wine list.

4. With white wines, the younger the better. As a basic rule, whites are best aged a couple of years; any older and they'll almost certainly have lost a little of their fruity zing. With reds you can go a year further back, as they age slightly better. Cheaper wines diminish with age, expensive wines improve – you remember that.

5. Cheap doesn't always mean inferior. It's often merely less fashionable. A South African sauvignon is far cheaper than one from New Zealand simply because it's less 'fashionable', though both taste equally good. Italian and Spanish grapes are also worth considering for the same reason.

6. With fish dishes of any kind ... you're safe with all whites and most of the cheaper end of the New World reds – those from Argentina, Australia and New Zealand, for example. But with reds, avoid anything containing tannin as it will taste metallic with the fish and you'll screw your face up as you eat.

7. Overchilling white wine paralyzes the taste. You can tell if it's too cold if the glass frosts up when it's poured. To remedy this, ask the wine waiter to remove the bottle from the ice bucket or cooler and shove it up hi ... er, and wait until it's warmed up before drinking. For this reason alone, wine should always be tasted before you eat (see below). If the food turns up before the wine – send it straight back with a contemptuous glare.

8. Never order wine without tasting it first. Make sure the bottle's opened in front of you to ensure it's the one you ordered. If the waiter opens the wrong bottle in front of you, it's your mistake rather than his. And if you don't like the taste of the wine you're trying but there's nothing actually wrong with it, you've chosen poorly and are expected to buy the bottle and learn from your mistake.

9. Send bad wine back. If a wine tastes oxidized (it'll be old, brown and particularly dull-tasting) or if it's corked (it smells musty and mouldy), send it straight back. Corked wine especially is still such a problem that you'll get one sooner or later and you won't be able to tell until the bottle's opened. Screw caps are replacing corks on many mid-priced wines, which helps, but even screw-cap wines need to be offered for slurping first as the wine may have been contaminated along the production line.

10. Buy champagne. If your only reason for ordering wine is to impress a date, buy champagne instead. Yes, sparkling wine from New Zealand is a lot cheaper, often better and made in exactly the same way, but nothing has quite the same effect on shallow ladies as a bottle of over-priced champagne (see page 73, How To ... Open Champagne (The Sophisticated, Unflustered Way)).

How To ...
Pull Off A Handbrake Turn

For those occasions when a gentle three-point-turn just won't suffice, you might want to unleash your inner stunt driver by pulling a quick handbrake turn instead. It's fairly easy to master ...

You'll need:

- A suitable car, preferably a front-wheel-drive model with a bit of poke and a 'lever and button-release' style handbrake. If the handbrake operates on the front wheels, find another car.
- A large open space – ideally a quiet, non-residential-type area where you won't get pinched. A damp or gravel surface will make it easier to pull off the turn and is less wearing on your tyres, although that shouldn't concern a maverick like you.
- A crowd of people drinking lurid green-and-blue paedopops, several of whom are wearing hoods and spitting indiscriminately. Otherwise, if nobody else witnesses your U-turn, what's the point of doing it?

You'll need to cruise along at a leisurely speed of around 30 to 35 mph – any slower and you'd struggle to complete the 180 degrees, any faster and your momentum could end up taking you backwards, for which you'll be marked down.

You should be in second gear at this point, with your favoured hand positioned so that it can give the wheel a full turn. The exact position depends on which way you want to turn: if you're turning the front end to the right, place your right hand on the left side of the wheel, at around the 7 o'clock position. If the car's going to the left, place the left hand on the right of the wheel, around the 5 o'clock mark. You're now about ready to pull your stunt, so this is how it should unravel:

Step 1. Grip the handbrake and keep the release button firmly pressed in, but don't pull it up quite yet.

Step 2. Let your foot come off the accelerator, then step on the clutch (and keep it floored until the car stops).

Step 3. Sharply turn the steering wheel, at least a half-turn in your chosen direction. Speed is of the essence, so make it a good sharp tug.

Step 4. A mere fraction of a second after turning the wheel, pull up the handbrake and you should feel the car's rear brakes lock the wheels, and then the rear end start to move/slide in a 'controlled oversteer'.

Step 5. At this point you and your car should be rotating, which is when you need to counter-steer the wheel back to a neutral position. Do it gradually so you end up with all four wheels pointing straight when you complete the turn.

You'll need to experiment with the moment at which

you release the handbrake – depress too quickly and you won't complete the turn, hold on too long and you'll over-cook it. Complex stuff such as vehicle weight, speed/velocity and road surface/conditions dictate, which is another way of saying you'll have to work out the release point for yourself.

Step 6. Apply the footbrake if you think the car will end up moving backwards. If all's gone to plan, you should now be facing the opposite direction. If you've got your tugs and turns all wrong and the car's upside down, on its side or just not fully turned, decide if you can be bothered to try again.

How To...
Break Down A Locked Door

Before Plod takes an active interest in this one, let's emphasize that you're breaking down the door in an emergency. There's a raging fire and you need to escape, or you fear that whoever's on the other side of the door requires some urgent medical attention, that kind of thing.

Under no circumstances should this skill be used for burglary, partly because that's illegal and partly because the technique you're about to learn involves planting your foot through the door as hard as you can, which would wake up every person in the street. If you're a burglar, you'd probably be better off waiting till after dark and then picking the lock.

The technique

A TV detective would run at the door, make contact with his shoulder and be through in no time, even if he was the type of flabby copper who gets out of breath walking up stairs. Think Tosh Lines from *The Bill*, God rest his soul. A proper copper. Now, clearly that technique can work, but only if you're a trained professional. For the amateur, the chances of you dislocating your shoulder are high and your momentum will carry you through the door and into the room – if there's a fire on the other side, you could well blunder into the flames and burn to a crisp.

The safer technique is to put your foot through the door's weak point, which is to the side of where the lock is mounted – the keyhole gives it away. With as much force as you can muster, you'll need to land a stout kick to the lock area. Kick just to the side of the lock rather than directly on it, unless you want to bugger up your foot.

Plant the underside of your foot as firmly as you can, using what can best be described as a half-arsed karate kick approach. Make a firm contact, push hard through the bottom of your foot and the wood should quickly splinter and the door fall open. If it doesn't, kick it again. And again. And again, if need be, particularly if it's a more sturdy exterior door. Eventually you'll get through, and danger will be averted.

How To...
Tie A Fat-Knot Tie

In formal situations – interviews, crown-court appearances and particularly at weddings – a shoddy little pea of a knot will mark you out as a shambling tramp of a man, the kind of character who'll end the night drinking wine from his shoe.

The fat Windsor knot, by contrast, is the choice of the debonair; the type of knot that purrs supreme confidence. It is, according to fictional ladies' man James Bond 'the mark of a cad', which we're taking to be a good thing. It is also, at the time of going to press, the knot of choice among professional footballers, which if nothing else illustrates how idiot-proof it must be to perfect.

Now, if you're quite ready, flip the collar of your shirt up and begin ...

Step 1. The fat end should extend about 30 cm below the thin end, hanging to your left as you look down. Cross fat end over thin and bring up through the loop between the collar and your tie; then feed it back down.

Step 2. Pull right so the fat end passes over your left index finger (which is holding the beginning of the knot in place), bring back behind the hand and up to the left, so the underside of the tie is now facing to the front.

Step 3. Bring the fat end across the front and to the right again, and at this point it should hook over the second finger on your left hand. Bring it under and up through the loop, then down through the by-now almost-formed knot in front.

Step 4. Tighten carefully and draw up to the collar, making sure it's not all lop-sided. Flip the collar back down, apply a splash of cologne and enjoy your textbook knot in the mirror for a few moments.

Some rules, but by no means a definitive list:

The Windsor works best with light fabrics such as silk (rather than heavy woollen ties that will have the knot sagging), and on wide-collared shirts where the knot can stretch out and breathe.

As a general rule, your tie should be darker than your shirt. If in doubt, look in the mirror and ask yourself a few searching questions.

A tie should hang just far enough to touch the waist on your slacks, which should be pulled up properly and not hanging around your arse like some snotty teen.

When it comes to removing the tie, reverse the four steps above to keep it in pristine condition. Rip it loose as fast as possible and you'll distort its shape.

How To...
Buy A Second-Hand Car

Now, no one's claiming that all second-hand car salesmen are confidence tricksters looking to swindle you out of your hard-earned savings, but there are always a few shysters who ruin it for the rest of them. Many second-hand car salesmen are a credit to their profession; their vehicles are reliable, comfortable and represent marvellous value for money. They are a great bunch of lads. The others are scumbags, hence this guide.

This is by no means the definitive list, because buying a second-hand car is a potential minefield of problems, but you'd be well advised to follow these lessons carefully before you consider swapping a large wad of cash for any set of keys.

Lesson 1. Do your homework

Before you go anywhere near a second-hand car, scour magazines and websites for information on the model(s) you have in mind. You'll have a better idea of what's included as standard, the going price for your chosen model and of any potential problems you may encounter with this type of car.

Lesson 2. Shop around

Once you've narrowed it down to a particular model, shop around to get the best price. Search through car-trade rag

Auto Trader and the local papers, and then visit several local dealers.

Lesson 3. Play detective

Once you've located the ideal car to suit taste and budget, investigate it further. Make sure it has a full service history, plus receipts to back the stamps up. Read through the previous receipts – this will show you any problems the car's had, as well as giving you an opportunity to check they've been rectified. If the car has been looked after, the owner will be proud to show you the paperwork. If he doesn't have the records and he makes a shabby excuse for why not, make your own excuses and leave.

Lesson 4. Look closely

Only ever view a second-hand car outdoors, in daylight and in dry weather – rain can hide many defects in paintwork. Stand about 5 metres away and look for any changes in panel colour, a sure sign of any previous accident damage. Every panel should be the same shade – any drips or blemishes suggest that it's had a respray. For the same reason, make sure the gaps between all panels look equal and flush. Uneven gaps between panels suggest they've been bolted back together after a crash. Excess paint around the window rubbers and under the wheel arches should set warning bells ringing, as should fresh paint marks in the boot or under the bonnet. How come you hadn't noticed the salesman's shifty eyes before now?

Lesson 5. Tread carefully

Check the tyres for uneven wear – it's often a sign that the steering and suspension are damaged and need adjusting

– at your expense. A new tyre comes with 8 mm tread depth, and the legal limit is 1.6 mm. Any less than that and you're breaking the law and inviting mishaps. A tread-depth gauge will cost you next to nothing and take an accurate reading.

Also, as a basic but generally reliable test, check to see if the tyres are all made by the same manufacturer. An owner who cares for his car will normally stick to the same brand.

Lesson 6. Drive on

Take the car out for a thorough test drive, perhaps packing a picnic and making a day of it through a nice country park. Once around the block will tell you bugger all about this motor – to give it a full road-test and check out its suspension and handling you'll need to be out for at least fifteen minutes driving on motorways, country roads, through built-up areas and on bumpy surfaces. Listen for any unusual engine noise, rattles and knocks, and push every button to make sure they are all in full working order. After the drive, check under the engine for any leaks or steam, and sniff for the ominous stench of burning.

Lesson 7. Call for help

If you're buying privately or without a warranty, have the AA or RAC inspect the vehicle for you. These men are trained, they know what to look for and, for around £200, they'll give you a detailed report and fewer sleepless nights. If they find something wrong that can be easily fixed, barter with the salesman to get some money off.

Lesson 8. Call for help again

According to figures by the independent vehicle-check

firm HPI, one in every twelve cars has been clocked – their mileage illegally altered by a scumbag in overalls. To check a car's previous form, including any insurance claims and it's true current value, make sure HPI check it over first (www.hpicheck.com) – it costs about £40. If you only do one thing on this list, make it this one.

Lesson 9. Buy local

Buying closer to home means you can return the car if there's a problem. If it's a dealer, he'll want to uphold his reputation, so selling you a dodgy motor is not a wise move. If it's a private sale you have less legal comeback, so be suspicious to the point of paranoia. Dodgy dealers sometimes sell privately to evade legal responsibility, while unscrupulous individuals will do all they can to cover their tracks. Beware private traders with several cars for sale, advertisers with mobile contact only, shifty individuals who give vague, evasive answers and twitch a lot. Only ever view at the seller's property so you know where to address any complaints. If he suggests meeting in a pub car park or some quiet country lane in the middle of nowhere, tell him to swivel.

Lesson 10. The golden rule

If in doubt about any aspect of the car, or the dealer, take your business elsewhere.

How To ...
Unblock The Toilet

It really couldn't be any easier, which makes you wonder why a plumber will charge you £50 just to come out, scratch his chin, shake his head and chirp: 'Dear oh deary me – buggered, innit?' before prodding around the U-bend with a stick for an extra £120 plus VA-sodding-T. Flabby twat. You'd be far better off fixing it yourself. Like so ...

How to fix it yourself

If the water level rises almost to the pan rim then drains very slowly, there's probably a blockage in the section of pipes your waste is flushed along, or the drain it discharges into. It's most likely a mix of excess toilet paper and a large manly deposit.

Never flush the toilet over and over in the hope that the blockage will just disappear on its own. It won't – and you'll get mucky water all over your bathroom floor. Instead, you'll need to force the water down the toilet to dislodge the blockage.

For this you'll need a plunger to create the pressure. Before you begin, scoop out any high water into a bucket, then take said plunger and insert into the bottom of the pan to block the outlet. Push down two or three times, firmly enough for a few splashes of murky toilet water to jump out. You're wearing a pair of long rubber gloves, so it won't matter, although it may smell slightly ripe.

If you have no plunger, a long-handled mop works fairly well. Failing that, a wire coat hanger unfurled can be poked down the toilet to probe round the bend. It's also said that a bread knife kept beside the toilet to cut up bulky waste also sorts the problem at source, but you should avoid using the knife to slice bread thereafter.

When the blockage has been dispersed, the water level should drop to normal. Flush to see if it's cleared properly. If it rises high again, repeat the process.

If it still doesn't clear, accept defeat and begrudgingly call a plumber. It could be that you'll need to clear the underground drain, which would involve fishing around in faeces. So why not let Oddjob earn his money for once?

How To ...
Put Yourself Out When You Catch On Fire

It's sadly inevitable that at some point in your life this will happen. One minute you're walking past a naked flame, the next you're ablaze and screaming 'Arggh, arggh, ooohh, arggh!' You'll need to act fast and think a little more calmly if you're to avoid becoming a huge fireball and burning to a crisp.

Flames need oxygen to survive, so running around is playing right into their fiery hands. You'll need to snuff the flames out by starving them of oxygen. The easiest way to do this is to jump into a river or have at least a dozen people simultaneously spit on you. Failing that, these three crucial steps could be your only hope ...

Step 1. Stop running around screaming like a girl. Stay calm and still.

Step 2. Drop down onto your front. This helps prevent the flames from spreading upwards to your face and head, where they'll do some serious damage to your pretty-boy features.

Step 3. Finally, roll on the ground to snuff the flames out. Deprive them of oxygen and they'll quickly die out.

Of course, if you discover someone else on fire, ensure they follow the above procedure, then help snuff out the flames by patting them down with a blanket or jumper at Step 3.

Disclaimer: like most of the entries in this book that involve potentially dangerous or life-threatening situations, this advice is to be used in genuine emergencies only, and not to bail out anyone who's been set alight as a prank.

How To ...
Iron A Shirt

Job interview, wedding, funeral, a date with the beak: there comes a time in every man's life when his appearance really matters, and when only a crease-free shirt will do. As with the rest of this book, we're working on the assumption that you can't get your mother or other half to do it for you, so here's all you need to know.

Preparation

First, check the label on your shirt so you know which material you're dealing with – some are more delicate than others, such as silk, although if you can afford to wear silk shirts you can afford to pay someone to wash, iron and hang your entire collection of shirts. And, to avoid confusing men like you and me, most iron manufacturers include handy symbols on their products which tally with the symbols on your shirt. Matching them up should be a doddle; linen setting for a linen shirt, cotton for cotton, etc. for etc., and so on. For the best results, iron the shirt when it's slightly damp to avoid creases and wrinkles setting into the material.

Before you begin, test your iron on the inside of your shirt (on a section that won't be visible when you're tucked in) to make sure it doesn't scorch a dirty great iron shape onto your garment. If you're doing more than one shirt, start with those which need a lower temperature and build up to the higher heat.

Ironing experts suggest that if you're working with a steam iron, distilled water is essential to avoid clogging the iron and leaving shabby sedimentary deposits all down your shirt, which will undermine all your hard work. Now, working on the inside of the shirt, iron in the following order ...

1. Collar and cuffs

Place the underside of the collar flat on the board and hold taut to avoid wrinkles, then iron from the outer points towards the centre – your best bet for avoiding creases. Repeat on the front of collar, then iron both sides of both cuffs.

2. Sleeves

Ensure the sleeve is flat on the board, elbow side first, and that the seam is aligned neatly at the sides. The seams are the most fiddly part to iron, but if you ignore them you'll look like you just couldn't be arsed to do it properly. Work up from the bottom of the arm to the top. Repeat on the other arm, then iron the fronts of both arms in the same manner while allowing your mind to wander onto something more interesting. Like cheese.

3. Back

Position the shoulder over the narrow, pointy end of the board and iron towards the centre, then repeat on the opposite shoulder. Now lay the back of the shirt flat on the board and iron out any creases in whatever style you see fit. Some experts suggest moving left to right across the shirt produces the best results, others claim right to left, but they're just waffling for the sake of it and it really doesn't matter. The end result should be that you remove any and all creases.

4. Front

Finally, flip the shirt over and lay one side of the front flat on the board. This is the most vital side as it'll be on view to anyone who pulls you up for a stop and chat, so even if you've rushed through stages 1, 2 and 3, take extra effort here. If the shirt has a pocket, start on that side and apply extra pressure around the buttonholes and between the buttons – if your iron's any good, it will have grooves which allow you to manoeuvre easily around them. Repeat any areas you missed or which still have creasing, then hang immediately or slip straight on – there are no hard or fast rules where this one's concerned. Just remember to turn off the iron, then to double-check an hour later when doubts begin to creep in.

If in doubt, cheat

For the man who's too bone idle to run an iron over his shirt, there is apparently another way, one which requires almost no effort at all. Before you clamber into the shower, hang the shirt just out of range of the water but close enough for the steam to penetrate its fibres. When the steam gets in, many of the creases will drop straight out (and onto the floor).

For even better results, albeit with a little more forethought and effort needed on your part, put the shirt on a hanger and button it up. Turn the shirt upside down and attach a clip hanger at the bottom – a clip hanger being one of those with clip attachment things at the bottom. Hang said shirt close to the shower, as before, but weigh it down by threading a heavy towel through the clip hanger's triangle. The added weight will pull the shirt taut and the tension on the fibres should stretch the creases out. You may need to shower for upwards of an hour to get every last crease out, but if it saves you the bother of ironing then who's complaining?

How To...
Dive Like Tarzan

The only problem here is that Tarzan had a penchant for diving head first off craggy cliff tops, which is far too dangerous to recommend to a novice. So, let's relocate to the swimming pool or the sea, and learn from the modern-day doyen of the dive: Mitch Buchanan of *Baywatch*.

Now, the 'Mitch Buchanan Hollywood Dive' is typically used to save drowning women in tight bikinis, with the hero dressed in nothing more than a pair of tight, cobbler-hugging swimming briefs. These are optional, but with your paunch you'd probably be better off wearing something with a more generous cut. What's not optional, however, is that unless you're trained in the ways of lifesaving, the MBHD should only ever be used to inject a little showmanship into your pool or sea entry. It should unfold as follows ...

The 'Mitch Buchanan Hollywood Dive'
Step 1. A smooth, controlled entry into the water is the key. Take a few steps as you run up, plant your weaker foot on the edge of the boat or side of the pool and push your body forward with your stronger foot. Really drive through with the push to get enough distance on the dive and avoid a tepid flop over the edge.

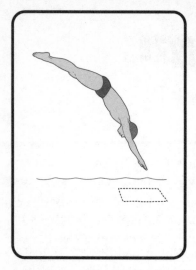

Step 2. Aim for a graceful 45-degree 'loop' up and down into the water, so that as your body dives forward, your arms should come together in front of you with both hands forming a 'V' position, thumbs locked into place. Your head should dip down comfortably, just far enough to give you a more streamlined entry into the water.

Step 3. As you dive, focus on a small square on the surface of the water. Your whole body needs to dive through that imaginary square, so it needs to remain as straight as possible throughout the dive. Your arms should be relaxed, but held with enough tension to keep them straight throughout.

Mitch would tell you that the square technique makes things easier as it keeps your body compact throughout and promotes a graceful arcing entry into the pool – rather than the bellyflop of a flabby, artless amateur. You'd be a mug not to listen.

How To...
Spit-Shine Shoes
(So You Can See Your Face In Them)

Any old buffoon can shine up a pair of shoes with polish and a brush, but only a select few have mastered the art of coughing up a thick globule of phlegm and buffing up a shoe so ferociously that it's like looking into a mirror, albeit a very black mirror designed to confuse. There's more than one good reason for that: it's unhygienic, it takes for ever and ultra-shiny shoes make you look like a ponce. But even so, for any would-be squaddies, City bankers or flouncing dandies who may be reading, here's how you achieve 'the look' ...

Step 1. Apply a medium-thick layer of paste over your chosen shoe (sports shoes are ill-advised, particularly white ones). A bog-standard black shoe polish from any supermarket will suffice, but a specialist polish with some reference to the military in its name gives better results. Let sit for five minutes while it dries.

Step 2. Wrap a soft, clean cloth around your index finger, stretched over so it's tight and smooth. Spit on it, applying enough saliva for the cloth to be wet but not dripping. You can use water, yes, but then how is that a spit-shine?

Step 3. Using a brisk, efficient circular motion, buff the dried polish until the wax starts to become nice and shiny. If it helps you work, imagine some jumped-up little sergeant major is barking orders into your lughole while calling your mother all manner of crude names, none of which are true. As far as you know.

Step 4. Still using the damp rag, apply a fine layer of polish in a circular motion until a hazy shine begins to appear. Keep building up the layers until you have a completely smooth surface, but on each application use less polish and less force so as not to rub away the layers beneath that you've already worked in.

Step 5. Repeat until you can finally see your gurning mug staring back, accepting that this could well take several hours, hours you will never get back and may one day later regret frittering away on something so trivial as shoe maintenance. Use a soft, clean cloth to give shoes one final buff, then move on to the next page.

How To...
Make A Baby Stop Crying

Change its nappy, put it to bed, feed it, pick it up, bounce it about aimlessly on your knee, put it down, insert dummy, remove dummy, sing to it, waggle a toy in its face, make odd gurgling noises, change its nappy again or just hand it back to its mother, shake head in shame and shuffle quietly to one side.

How To ...
Use A Cut-Throat Razor

When it came to slashing customers' throats, popular nineteenth-century barber Sweeney Todd put his faith in the cut-throat razor – one quick slash of the trusty blade and the unfortunates were ready to be turned into rancid pies by 'Mad' Marge Lovett, his hoary accomplice. The customers he didn't butcher left his shop after the closest shave of their life, and to this day whisker experts declare the cut-throat (known also as the straight razor) to be the best a man can get. It remains highly dangerous, so approach with caution ...

Before you begin

Rinse your face with hot water to soften your whiskers, open the pores and ensure a closer shave. Lather the shaving area with shaving cream, preferably glycerine-based, using a circular motion with the bristles of the brush to lift the hairs and produce a rich, creamy lather. Experts suggest a badger-hair shaving brush works best, although badgers recommend a ferret-hair brush. Prepare the skin properly and the blade will glide across your face and give you a closer shave.

The shave

Step 1. Open the razor by gently gripping the handle with your thumb and three fingers. With the open handle pointing away from the face, place your little finger in the crook of the blade for a secure grip. The angle of the blade is dependent on the contours of your mug, but experts suggest you start at a 30-degree angle.

Step 2. Which part of your face you shave first is your call, but it's vital to hold the skin taut with your free hand – by creating a flatter surface the blade will glide more smoothly. As you shave, each stroke of the blade should follow the grain of your whiskers and run smoothly for 3 to 4 centimetres at a time.

Step 3. When you've shaved the whole beard, re-lather and start again. The smoothest shaves take two goes, but this time the strokes of the blade should run against the grain of the beard.

Step 4. After two shaves your face should be as smooth as the day you were born, but hopefully less bloody. Rinse with cold water and apply a moisturizing balm. In preparation for next time, rinse the razor thoroughly with hot water, wipe dry and store out of the reach of children and demented barbers.

Bloody hell

For any minor nicks along the way, apply a moistened alum block to the cut. This magical soap-sized block possesses blood-vessel-constricting astringent properties to curb any minor blood loss. A styptic pencil does a similar job, and both are far more effective than plastering toilet roll all over your face.

How To...
Rip A Phone Book In Half With Your Bare Hands

Even if you're a 6-foot-3-inch streak of piss with stick arms and the strength of an arthritic old lady, you will be able to pull this one off. Your build is irrelevant, writes a 6-foot-3-inch streak of piss with etc. etc., as it's all down to a combination of technique and chicanery. The trick is simply to break the spine* – once that's ripped, those flimsy pages will offer far less resistance.

The spineless approach
First, grip the book by its spine with both hands 3 to 4 centimetres apart. Your index fingers should be close together and along the top face of the book, with both thumbs along the bottom.

Bend the binding back and forth until it begins to tear, and then bend it back so the spine is straight again. Hold the book close into your body, around the stomach area and with your arms bent at 90 degrees – hold it at arms' length and it's far harder to gain the purchase and power needed to break through that spine.

Now, in one brisk movement, tear down the rip in the spine and through the pages in one sharp movement, to leave yourself with two halves of a phone book. Quite what you're going to do with two tatty halves of a phone book is not an issue for here and now.

A half-baked cheat's guide

If you need to weaken the spine further before attempting to rip through it, shove it in the oven at a very high temperature and bake for a few minutes until it crumbles slightly in your fingers. Allow to cool and the pages should be dry and brittle enough to rip through with little resistance. Nobody need ever know.

Professional phone-book rippers consider breaking the spine to be a cop-out option, as they tear through the pages first and finish at the spine. However, unless you have any ambition to turn professional, let's agree that they can shove their rules up their holes.

How To ...
Make A Bow And Arrow

This entry is still labouring under the notion that one day you'll be pitched into a big forest with nothing to survive on but your wits. However, it's far more likely that a young person will ask you to whittle him a bow and arrow like a proper dad should, instead of showing him the six-month pre-record feature on your new DVD recorder. Either way, the following instructions should just about cover the basics ...

Building a bow

Yew is traditionally the wood of choice, although in theory any old piece of wood will make a bow as long as it provides enough tension when you tighten the string. Find a six- (yes, six) foot pole or branch, preferably one that's not too green, and place one end on the ground.

Take a sharp implement, ideally an axe or anything that will trim down the branch, and taper the stick from the centre to the end – it should be thicker and sturdier in the centre, and fat enough for your hand to grip firmly. Taper in the same fashion towards the other end, cutting nocks (small indents) for the string in both ends with a knife.

Take a length of string, attach it to both ends and tighten so the bow becomes taut and gives you a decent twang. Animal sinew, bark from certain trees and even resilient nettles would also work, but string's much easier. You now have yourself a working bow.

Adding the arrows

Unlike the knobbly bow, your arrows have to be made more accurately if they're to fly straight. You'll need a few lengths of reed or bamboo, and each piece needs to be as straight as possible.

Even then, the chances are your wonky, would-be arrow won't be straight enough to use, so you'll need to hold it over a fire until the wood softens, allowing you to bend and straighten it by hand. Use your generic whittling tool to smooth it out as much as possible and to reduce its drag through the air. Now make several more, otherwise every time you fire your solitary arrow you'll need to chase after it and find it.

Cut a nock at one end and glue a small feather a couple of centimetres or so down the shaft to make the arrow fly straighter and look more professional. Finally, sharpen to a point at the other end so that when you fire it from the bow it will stick in all manner of woodland vermi ... what? Ah. The Woodland Police say you're not allowed to shoot rodents, not even if you're living in the woods, starving hungry and with no one around to miss this critter. So, as a slightly disappointing alternative ending, add a small blob of Plasticine to the tip to aid flight and satisfy all health and safety guidelines.

How To...
Fire A Bow And Arrow*

First, a further word of warning from the Countryside Police: you're not allowed to fire any form of arrows at small furry creatures in Great Britain – you're not a redneck and our creatures are free to roam without fear of being shot up the arse with a wonky stick.

Should you wish to fire a bow and arrow, perhaps using the one you made on the previous pages, focus instead on a big circular board or a tin can on a wall, then set yourself up like so ...

Step 1. Stand side-on to your target with your feet about shoulder's width apart and your toes facing forwards, but with the tips of the shoes forming an imaginary line down towards the centre of the target.

Step 2. Place the notched end of the arrow on the string so it sits comfortably, and hold in place so that the arrow rests between the index and middle fingers of your dominant hand.

Step 3. Hold the bow grip with your other hand and allow the far end of the arrow to rest on the top of the hand, just above the knuckle. Beginners might like to wear a glove for extra safety.

Step 4. Bring the bow arm up to shoulder height, and draw the string back in a straight, horizontal line, keeping both shoulders as low as possible and with your shoulder blades moving towards each other. Stay relaxed as you focus on the target.

Step 5. Pull back the string as far back as the middle of your chin. Your index finger should rest beneath the chin. Your bow hand, your draw hand (the one pulling the string) and your elbow should form as straight a line as possible, with the back muscles remaining tense and both shoulders kept as low as possible. Keep the bow arm slightly bent out, away from the path of the string.

Step 6. Aim with the eye that's furthest from the target, and shut the other to focus. Keep the point of the arrow aimed at the target, elevating it slightly to compensate for distance – the further away the target, the higher you'll need to aim to compensate for the arrow losing height as it travels.

Step 7. Steady your body and the shot by closing your mouth, clamping your teeth together and holding your breath. Pull back the string – the further you pull the further it will fly, unless you pull too far and it snaps (in which case, turn back to the previous entry). Release the string and the arrow should, in theory, twang off towards the target.

Step 8. Keep aiming at the target until the arrow has struck. For extra artistry points and a more dramatic flourish, when you release the string your draw hand should be near or behind your ear.

Step 9. Now, with the next arrow, coat the head in paraffin, set fire to it and launch it onto the nearest thatched roof.

Step 10. No, hold on. The Fun Police say you can't do that either. Balls.

These instructions are based on firing a longbow only; other bows require different techniques. They're good for both left- and right-handed gents, though.

How To...
Jump-Start A Car

You can swear at your car all you like, but *it* didn't leave the lights on overnight or while you were at work all day, so if anyone's an 'effing tossbag' in this sorry episode, it's probably you.

But it doesn't matter, because having read this entry you know the importance of carrying a set of jump leads in your boot. They're available from all half-decent car accessory shops and will resuscitate a drained battery in minutes. You know better than to jump-start a frozen battery, of course, for it will explode. But that's another matter altogether.

As well as the leads, you'll need a friend with a healthy car, or a stranger kind enough to let you fish about under his bonnet and drain his battery for fifteen minutes. You'll need to check both manuals to ensure the batteries are the same voltage and both jump-start-friendly, but you're not stupid and would have done that anyway. And if all tallies, you're about ready …

Step 1. Position the good car next to the bad before switching off both ignitions and all electrical equipment. Apply both handbrakes and put the cars into neutral (or P for automatics), and, to avoid an explosion, extinguish any cigarettes, pipes or cheroots before opening both bonnets. The cars should be close enough to comfortably attach the leads, but never touching – unless you want to scratch the paintwork and risk sparks or a giant blast.

Step 2. On the bad car (although we're not blaming him, it wasn't his fault), connect one end of the red jump lead to the positive terminal on the battery, marked with an idiot-proof '+' sign. Attach the other end to the positive terminal on the good car's healthy battery, making sure that as you move the wire across it doesn't touch any metal on the vehicle, including (obviously) the bodywork.

Step 3. Now take the black jump lead and connect one end to the negative ('–') terminal of the good battery and the other end to any unpainted metal surface under the bonnet on the bad vehicle, providing it's well away from the battery, fuel systems, carburettor or any moving parts. Never connect this end to the negative terminal on the bad battery, otherwise both will explode, and then you're buggered. Also, never touch negative and positive clamps together or you'll destroy both batteries. And beware of any small sparks flying, which may make you yelp like a small child.

Step 4. Wait three minutes for the voltages to equalize before starting the good car up and letting it run for a minute or so, then start the bad car up and run both at a fast (but idle) speed for ten minutes. If you don't keep the leads connected throughout, you risk damaging the cars' electronics.

(If your engine still won't start, turn off the engine, readjust the red clamp by either reattaching or turning it for a better connection and start again. If it still fails, your problem may run deeper than a flat battery and you'll need to call out the expensive men in overalls.)

Step 5. Ten minutes later, turn off the ignition on both cars and disconnect the leads in reverse order. Be careful not to undo all your good work by touching the clips against each other, yourself or the car's bodywork.

Step 6. If successful, restart your engine and flick on the lights, the heated rear window and the heater to prevent any voltage surges. You'll need to keep your car running for at least half an hour to recharge the battery, whether it's sat revving away in a car park or back on the road. When you do finally drive off, take great care not to stall, and be aware that draining your battery like that won't have done it any good. It may be prudent to drive straight to a garage to have it checked over or replaced. That might teach you to take more care next time.

How To ...
Perform The Kiss Of Life

The Grim Reaper has his paws all over another victim and is working fast, so there's no time to stand around scratching your chin and deliberating over possible remedies.

The victim has stopped breathing and appears to have no pulse. In this situation it's usually a cardiac arrest, most commonly caused by a heart attack, most commonly caused by doughnuts, cheese and slothful ways. If the heart stops beating normally, oxygen can't be pumped around the body effectively. Without meaning to put a downer on the book, when that happens damage to the brain occurs after four minutes, which becomes irreversible after seven and permanent after fifteen. So look sharp ...

The kiss of life – aka CPR
(or cardiopulmonary resuscitation)

If the victim is unresponsive, he won't react if you shout or prod him. To check, ask him loudly if he's OK ... If he doesn't respond, you'll need to follow the most basic 'ABC' routine. Check his airway ('A') is clear by tilting his head back and lifting his chin forward, then look in his mouth for any obstructions (including his own tongue). Check for breathing ('B') by looking and listening for any chest movement. Finally, check for indications of blood circulation ('C'), by feeling for any signs of a pulse – the wrists and neck are the easiest places to identify a pulse. The ABC procedure should take no more than ten seconds to perform and if there's no response, call the ambulance (tel: 999) before performing CPR, just in case the worst comes to the worst. The first few minutes are critical to help keep the key organs alive until the ambulance arrives or the victim begins to show clear signs of recovery. CPR for adults is a combination of chest compressions and rescue breaths. CPR for kids is detailed afterwards.

Step 1. Chest compressions

Lie the victim on his back, providing he can be safely moved into position without sustaining injury. With your hands placed in the middle of the chest, right between the nipples and with one on top of the other, push down firmly to perform one chest compression.

Press down between 4 and 5 cm, aiming to pump at a rate of 100 compressions every minute, i.e. faster than one every second. This alone could revive the victim, though you might hear a sharp cracking sound. That's just his cartilage or ribs cracking, but when the alternative is death he can't really complain. If thirty chest compressions don't rouse him, prepare to give him two rescue breaths.

Step 2. Two rescue breaths

Tilt the head back to open the airway, then pinch the victim's nose, cover their mouth with yours and blow for a second, until you see the chest rise. Give another quick breath, again lasting only a second, then apply thirty more chest compressions.

If there is no reaction, repeat the procedure. If the breaths are successful, the victim will cough and splutter and may even show their appreciation by vomiting on you. Turn their head to the side so they don't choke, wipe away as much vomit as possible and continue with CPR, or see if someone else wants to take over from here. No takers? Continue until the person begins to breathe normally and the ambulance arrives carrying the experts who can finish the job. If you got the victim this far, you can feel very proud of yourself.

One for the kiddies

These instructions remain much the same for children and babies, apart from that you should begin with five rescue breaths, and then revert to cycles of thirty compressions and two breaths. Use only one hand (assuming he's smaller than you) to make the compressions, and just two fingers for a baby.

How To ...
Build A Fire

When roaming the great outdoors in search of manly adventure and a few of life's big answers, you'll no doubt need to bunk down for the night, preferably around a roaring fire. The warmth could keep you alive if it's a particularly nippy night, plus it also allows you to cook and eat any beasts you've caught during the day. That's the needless scene-setting taken care of, here's how to construct the world's simplest fire ...

Burn, baby, burn

You'll need a fire that's quick and easy to assemble, and there's none more quick or easy than the Tepee Fire. As the name suggests, it's shaped like a tepee, and built to allow enough oxygen in to burn the fuel but also to protect the flames from the wind.

Begin by feeling the ground. If it's wet, scatter a bed of dry leaves and twigs to keep the fuel as dry as possible until the flames have been established. Then construct as follows ...

Step 1. Place the dry tinder (dead grass, straw, wood shavings, feathers, anything small that will burn) in the centre and build up a few small sticks of kindling (twigs and strips of wood, dry pine cones broken up into small pieces, or dry leaves) into a small tepee over the top. The kindling should be no smaller than a matchstick and no bigger than a pencil, positioned so there's enough space to insert your hand to light the fire and to allow it to breathe. Keep a bumper supply of kindling to add onto the fire as it burns, keeping it as dry as possible for very obvious reasons.

Step 2. Unless you're lighting with two sticks (see page 28), strike a match and hold it downwards for a moment to allow the flame to stabilize and burn. Touch the flame on the tinder bundle and carefully place (never throw) on extra kindling until the fire builds up nicely. As the tepee burns, the outer logs will fall inwards, feeding the fire. Keep adding the smaller wood, then apply the bigger, bulkier bits.

Step 3. If you run out of dry wood, dried grass twisted into bunches and dried animal dung burn very well indeed, and no man should leave home without the latter.

Safety issues

If you build a fire beneath long, overhanging branches or close to bushes, you could soon have a much larger fire on your hands than originally planned. Clear a patch of ground before you begin.

If the wind is whipping in and causing no end of troubles, dig down into the ground to create a sheltered fire pit. Use your hands and any sharp implements available to create a pit 1 foot deep by about 2 feet wide, then build your tepee at a lower, more protected level. Have a pile of soil on hand to snuff out the fire, just in case it spreads out of control, and clear up all that mess before you move on.

How To ...
Stage-Dive

Aren't you a bit old for all that nonsense?

How To ...
Win An Arm-Wrestle

Luckily, you don't need to be six foot tall and full of muscle to win an arm-wrestling encounter: speed, technique and strategy are as vital as pure strength. The key is to hit your opponent so fast that by the time he's cottoned on to what just happened, you're showered, changed and enjoying a celebratory drink in the bar.

Top-rolling is the simplest and most effective technique in arm-wrestling, providing you get it right. This method is not about the biceps and forearms, but rather a battle of hand, finger and wrist strength. Your aim is to force intense pressure on your opponent's hand – this will 'open up' his grip and allow you to strengthen yours. Denied the power he needs, you're in position to go in for the kill and touch his arm down on the table. This is how the whole episode should, in theory, unfold ...

The set-up

Make a fist in front of you, with the top of your thumb and the nail facing towards your nose – the thumb should about 20 cm away from your nose. The line from your shoulder to your elbow (essentially the bicep) should be behind your forearm – if it's in front, your arm is already heading backwards, towards inevitable defeat.

Look down at your index finger; the first two knuckles should be facing high towards the ceiling as you make the fist. If you imagine a horizontal line between those two knuckles, you'll be attempting to pull that line towards your nose. Despite what you may think, there's absolutely no sideways pushing in arm-wrestling. You only ever try to maintain the position of your arm in its strength 'sweet spot' (the start position) and then pull backwards towards your body, as if pulling a pint of ale.

Your arm and body should remain in that 'optimum position' and only ever move as one. The arm will

Main image: *The basic grip and set-up (opponent clearly not pictured).* Smaller image: *Re-grip high up to weaken your opponent's grip.*

obviously move – preferably to the left as you close in on victory – but the angles of wrist and fingers need to remain in position throughout, otherwise you'll lose power and risk an arm-twanging injury.

The technique

With the top-roll, your aim is to beat your opponent by rolling his wrist backwards and his arm over. This is apparently simple enough.

When you hear the words 'Ready, Go', you're off. Pull back your arm very smoothly. Never jerk the arm in an attempt to finish your opponent off quickly, as you're more likely to bugger up that 'optimum position' mentioned earlier. Force his arm towards you and away from his body and you disrupt his 'optimum position'. Work fast to gain greater leverage and build on your advantage. If his grip loosens, try to walk your fingers out, re-grip higher up his hand and then work them out a little bit more. Keep going and you'll eventually have enough leverage to take him down.

A word of warning

In the unlikely event that he somehow gets the upper hand, make sure your shoulder and your whole body stay with your arm and move in the same direction. Don't ignore everything you've just learnt and apply a desperate sideways yank of the arm. Keep the pressure consistent and chip away at his grip to turn the pressure back on him. If you retain your optimum position, dig deep into your reserves and psyche him out with 'the evil eye', you've probably got the beating of your opponent.

How To ...
Fend Off A Dangerous Beast

Most animals you encounter during your lifetime will be of the cuddly or fluffy variety: kittens and ponies and little bunny rabbits with big floppy ears who want nothing more than to rub their little nose against yours. But what about the nasty bastard animals that prefer to bite, trample and shred you to death? How do you escape unscathed when they attack? Luckily, this rough guide to surviving four of the most common psycho animal attacks might just save your bacon ...

A snappy, snarling dog

Now not all dogs are bastards, but because you can never tell until one snaps and goes for your throat, it pays to approach them all with suspicion.

The golden rule is: never approach a strange dog, particularly not on its own turf and never if it's eating, sleeping, chewing anything or surrounded by puppies. Most dogs will only bite as a last resort. They'll bark, growl and puff out their chests as a way of defending their patch and telling you to move on, but it's usually no more than bravado.

If the hound keeps its distance or backs away from you, it views you as more dominant and knows better than to attack.

If it lollops over, its tail wagging and big, slobbery tongue hanging out, you should be safe enough. He only wants to lick your hand and sniff your privates. This one poses no threat.

If, however, it approaches all snarly, staring at you with its tail held high, he fancies a piece of you. The worst thing you can do is turn on your heels and scarper, or even walk quickly away – a dog's natural instinct is to give chase.

Back off very slowly, facing the dog and showing no fear. Dogs can read fear in your eyes and your movement. They're also paranoid enough to feel threatened if you stare into their eyes, so avoid making eye contact. And if they catch you smiling at them, even nervously, a dog sees you baring your teeth and thinks you're up for a ruck.

Stay calm, talk to the dog firmly, perhaps complementing it on its lovely glossy coat and powerful-looking teeth, and back away from its patch very slowly.

That might be enough, but if the worst comes to the worst and the dog attempts to snap his jaws down on you, you'll need to shove something in its mouth for it to bite on: a coat, umbrella or suitcase would do; just anything that's not full of blood and attached to your body.

If you have nothing suitable to hand, feed it your arm, preferably wrapped in a thick sleeve to soften the pain. If the choice is between feeding the arm, or the dog jumping at your throat or knocking you down and attacking your head, why, that's no choice at all. Turn your arm so that it's biting down on the outer part rather than the underside, where all the important arteries are on offer. If he bites, don't try to struggle free – that's exactly what angry dogs with powerful snappy jaws want. He'd win in a straight tug and do terrible damage to your arm in the process.

Instead of pulling out, push your hand, fist or arm into its mouth to block its airway, make it gag and confuse its brain. This is a last resort, as is prodding the dog in the eyes with your free hand. If the choice is a severely gnawed hand/arm or a little discomfort to an angry uptight mutt, don't hesitate to push it, prod it and even punch it if it makes it stop. There really is no code of conduct when it comes to fighting dogs.

And finally, because this incident has already gone on far too long, if he knocks you over and has the choice of what to bite on, remain as calm and motionless as possible. Roll up into a tight ball with your hands over your ears (dogs like eating pigs' ears and yours won't taste dissimilar) and protect your throat with your knees. If he doesn't grow bored by your lifeless body and continues to attack, feed him the arm and prepare to fight dirty.

Survive a shark attack

Statistically, you're more likely to be stung on the arse by a bee than attacked by a shark, but there are always a few bad apples that spoil it for the rest of them by biting, maiming and eating swimmers. Great Whites, Tiger, Bull and Oceanic Whitetip sharks all have a history of bothering humans, so do your homework before venturing into their neighbourhoods.

According to experts, many shark attacks are merely a case of mistaken identity. They think you're plankton, take a bite and scarper when you taste wrong, confused and fearful of the threat you present. And, according to those same experts who've dedicated their lives to studying this subject, if you're unfortunate enough to be on the end of a sustained attack, your best bet is to get out of the water. Really. It's as simple as that.

On most occasions, the first the victim knows of an attack is when the beast comes from nowhere and bites hard on one of their body parts. If you can't clamber out of the water in time, your best bet is to fight back.

Prod and poke their most sensitive areas – the eyes and the gills – like your life depended on it, using any weapon you have to hand. Hit him on the nose if you can't reach the eyes and gills, but be aware that the nose is attached to its mouth, which is full of razor-sharp teeth.

If he attacks then backs off, he may well be waiting for you to die from any injuries he's inflicted. Use the time to plot your route out of the water, but be prepared to defend yourself again. If you're lucky, by denying a shark the upper hand, he's more likely to back down, bugger off and bother someone else instead.

Sidestep an angry bull

It's said that he won't bother you unless you bother him, so stay out of his field and you'll be all right. The end.

But what if you have no choice but to trample across his patch? All you can do here is give him as wide a berth as possible, walking calmly and confidently at a brisk, business-like pace.

If he starts to take an interest and you can run to safety, do so as fast as your legs will carry you. That said, never leg it without working out your distances: most bulls running at full pelt can move quicker than you and will toss you in the air and trample you underfoot.

If it's all too late and he's making those nasal snorts and scraping his front foot on the ground, your only hope is to make like a matador and whip off your coat or shirt. Bulls are big and powerful with sharp horns, but they're essentially gullible beasts who focus on movement. Hold an item of clothing to one side at arm's length and it will confuse and distract him.

Stand perfectly still and wait. If he charges, toss your makeshift cloak away from you once the bull has got within fifteen feet. He'll follow the cloak rather than you, and then become confused by what just happened. This can buy you time to make good your escape.

However, if you're some way from safety, you may have to steal several yards and then repeat the process: take off another item of clothing and confuse him again. Repeat this until you reach the safety of a fence, by which point you could be down to your underpants, which may well be soiled.

An alternative school of thought suggests that a bull can be controlled by grabbing its nose ring and twisting it sharply. Only a moron would try this, and while you may be lacking in certain skills, you're not a moron.

Wrestle an alligator

The easiest way to avoid being clamped between the jaws of a 'gator is to avoid holidaying in Florida and decline any invitation to go out on a small boat across a swamp. We've seen films and know how this one ends.

Most alligators are afraid of humans and prefer the safety of water, but they'll still nip out onto land if you show them a leg. If they want to be left alone and you've ventured into their territory, alligators open their mouths and hiss. Don't make him tell you twice – back away rapidly.

The alligators who want to eat you, on the other hand, are likely to emerge from the cover of water at anything up to 30 mph. If he catches you unaware, your best bet is to engage in what's known as a Manly Struggle.

The alligator wants to clamp his jaws down on you, drag you into the water and perform his Death Roll – where he shakes you around until bits of you fall off in bite-sized chunks.

Your only hope is to get on its back as fast as possible, apply downward pressure to its neck so that it can't take a bite, and pray a warden with a big gun comes to your rescue.

If the alligator manages to clamp down on a limb, a firm punch to the snout will open up his jaw and allow you to reclaim your body part.

Some experts suggest you cover his eyes as this can make alligators more sedate, while singing a gentle lament into its ear may also help. But if you only remember one thing from this entry, it should be: keep its jaws shut by applying pressure to its neck and remain on top until help finally arrives. And praying wouldn't hurt, either.

How To...
Tie The Trustiest Knots

Sadly, there is no one-knot-for-all-occasions, just many, many knots that do a number of different jobs. There are at least 350 decent fastenings in existence at the moment, so what follows here are three key knots useful in three important scenarios. Sadly, there wasn't room to include the Corned Beef Knot – used to keep corned beef together during cooking – or the Tarbuck Knot – a non-jamming knot, used by climbers and quite possibly named in honour of gap-toothed Scouse entertainer Jimmy Tarbuck.

A knot to secure stuff

The next time you need to take a cumbersome object from one place to another on top of your car (a suitcase, or tree, perhaps), secure it firmly using possibly the easiest

Thread as shown and cross the two ends (fig. 1). Feed both ends back round and through the loop, then pull both evenly to tighten (fig. 2).

fastening ever created: the Reef Knot. Devised by fishermen, this one's so simple that a twelve-year-old Cub Scout is expected to be able to tie it in his sleep, and should therefore be the default knot of every proper Man.

A knot to tie two ropes together

If you're about to abseil heroically down the side of a building,* look no further than the Double Fisherman's Knot (it being well known that many fishermen like to abseil down buildings in their spare time). It's suitable for tying two lengths of rope together (of either equal or unequal thickness, which is very useful), easy to apply but a right bugger to untie afterwards – and that's a good thing as it's less likely to suddenly unravel at 100 metres.

Overlap both ends (fig. 1), then wrap one end round both ropes, giving two full turns (figs 2 and 3) before feeding through and pulling tight (fig. 4).

Repeat with the other end (figs 5–8) before pulling on both ends to tighten securely.

*We can't recommend this. The Double Fisherman's Knot will work just as well for towing a car and lengthening a fishing line, both of which are far safer pursuits.

A knot to tie a robber up while you wait for the fuzz

Having tonked the intruder over the head with a piece of wood or a cheap ornament, two small birds should now be gently twittering above his slumped body. When he comes round in a few minutes he'll either scarper into the night or stove your head in and steal your life savings from the biscuit tin under your bed, so you'll need to restrain him until the policemen arrive.

Your best bet is to sit him in a stout chair and tie both wrists together with an ultra-secure Constrictor Knot; a loop far easier to apply than it is to undo. Add another Constrictor to each ankle, and warn him that he could do himself some serious damage by attempting to force his hands or legs free. Of course, when the police do finally show up they'll arrest you for GBH and let him off with a caution, for the law is indeed an arse.

Form a loop with the rope (fig. 1), then continue twisting until the line becomes a figure of eight (fig. 2). Twist further until the two ends of the figure of eight become individual loops (fig. 3). Place both loops over the hands and tighten (fig. 4). Act fast, in case he comes round.

How To...
Throw Properly
(And Not At All Like A Big Frilly Girl)

It doesn't matter what you're throwing, be it a slobbery tennis ball for a dog or some stones at your neighbour's greenhouse, your manly credentials are on the line with this one.

When throwing anything, anywhere, you'll be judged on two things: distance travelled by the hurtling object and the ability to complete the chuck without looking like a frilly tart. The following five steps are designed to make sure you score well on both counts ...

Step 1. Select your target and stand sideways to it, feet roughly shoulder-width apart to provide a stable base. If you're right-handed, the left foot and arm should both point towards the target, with the arm raised to shoulder height and providing balance. (Obviously you'll need to reverse this if you're left-handed.)

Step 2. Take the throwing arm up at a right angle to around shoulder height. With the non-throwing arm still focusing on the target, both arms should form an 'L' shape.

Step 3. Now, as the throwing arm swings forward, keep your elbow at least level with the top of the throwing shoulder. As the weight moves from the back to the front foot, release the ball as the body swings round and the chest faces the target. The perfect trajectory for distance is around 45 degrees, any higher and you'll gain height but lose distance, any lower and the object's arc will be too flat for it to travel far.

Step 4. To avoid the powder-puff finish, when the ball has been released the throwing arm should continue down and across the body so that it finishes next to the hip. If maximum force has been applied, the aiming arm should come down to finish behind the body.

Step 5. If you need extra distance, take a short run up, but make sure you remain balanced and your head stays still and focused on the target right up until the moment it makes contact. A textbook throw. Nothing even slightly girly about that.

How To...
Navigate By The Stars*

An ancient and fail-safe navigational trick practised by salty old mariners and alcoholics who wake up at the bottom of hedges. Should you ever find yourself lost in the middle of nowhere, look up to the night sky, wait for your eyes to focus and try to remember which hemisphere you're looking at. This will help you make sense of it all ...

If you're lost in the northern hemisphere

Look up and locate two constellations – Ursa Major (aka the Plough, the Big Dipper, the Great Bear and the Saucepan) and Cassiopeia. Ursa Major is a seven-star constellation shaped a bit like a farmer's plough, vaguely like a large ladle, nothing at all like a big bear and most of all like a

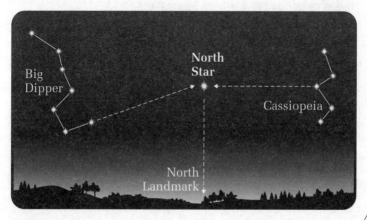

long-handled saucepan. Cassiopeia is less imaginative; it's merely five stars that form a 'W' shape hanging vertically.

Both will be visible on a clear night and always sit opposite each other and rotate around the vital North Star (aka Polaris, or Pole Star) – a star that points northwards, funnily enough.

To locate the North Star, find the two stars on the right-hand side of the Saucepan. These are 'pointer stars', so-called because if you draw an imaginary line between the two, and then extend that distance roughly five times again, the line should reach the North Star. To make certain, before stumbling off due west and into a swamp, check that the North Star is in line with Cassiopeia's centre star – the middle peak on the 'W'.

If this all tallies, locate true north by drawing an imaginary line back down vertically from the North Star to earth, and focus the base of the line on some kind of landmark. That way is north, directly behind you is south and the rest you really ought to be able to work out for yourself.

If you're lost in the southern hemisphere

This is trickier as there are no obvious cooking utensils by which to navigate. Instead, you'll need to find the Southern Cross – four bright stars forming a cross which looks like it's fallen over on its left side. Once located, its pointer stars are the two which would form the long shaft of the cross. To find south, take the distance between the two stars and project it five times as far, moving from left to right. Where the imaginary line ends, draw a line vertically straight down to the horizon and select a landmark to follow. Done correctly, you now have your bearings and can adjust accordingly. Walk on.

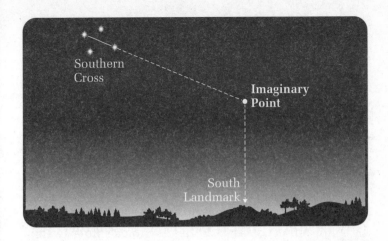

Though the position of the stars in the night sky depends on your location in the world and the time of year you are observing them, the arrangement of these constellations in relation to each other remains constant. You remember that.

How To...
Jump From A
Speeding Train

Sadly, How To ... Fight On Top Of A Speeding Train Like They Used To In The Old Days didn't quite make the cut, but the classic 'tumble from a train' was a shoo-in. It used to be that heroic men had no choice but to fling themselves from trains to avoid crash-based carnage or escape a man with a gun who wanted them dead. These days you're more likely to use this skill to avoid a jobsworth ticket inspector, but be aware that you can't just go flinging yourself off willy-nilly.

Our lawyers are very keen for us to stress that there is no absolutely safe way for average men to jump from a moving train. What there is, though, is the stuntman approach, which minimizes the risk of landing on your head or snapping both legs on impact.

You'll need the train to be travelling at no more than 20 mph, otherwise you'll end up dead. And you'll need to be jumping from a doorway not a roof, otherwise you'll also end up dead. Apart from that it's a breeze ...

The take-off point

A door is normally best for your exit, and preferably an open one. You need enough room to take a small running jump and a doorway wide enough to get through comfortably. When you push off from your take-off point, make sure your foot is firmly planted to provide you with a good, solid purchase. It will need to push you far enough out of the doorway so that you land safely away from the train rather than on the tracks.

The target

As you stand at the take-off point, visualize your own little landing zone further down the line. If you've any sense, make it an area free from rocks, fencing and farmyard animals – delay your jump until soft dirt and a flat surface draws into view. The very best you can hope for is a haystack, or failing that a small, soft, grassy hillock with a slight downward slope away from the tracks. That slope will lessen the impact on contact.

The take-off proper

When you jump, prepare to hit the ground and roll. Land as a parachutist would to cushion the impact: feet together, knees slightly bent, body mildly turned in the air towards the side you want to land on. After that, it's a case of 'assholes and elbows', according to those in the know. Whatever rolling skills you've picked up over the years will now inevitably take over.

Alternatively, if you approach the take-off point and realize that this wasn't one of your brighter ideas, stop, wait for the train to reach the next platform, alight as normal and pay the fine. Your choice.

How To ...
Barbecue Like A Man

Most men are drawn to hot coals like flies round a dog tart, yet only a small number know how to barbecue correctly. By correctly, we mean ensuring the meat comes out cooked properly and that none of the guests leaves early because you've poisoned them. Let's start at the beginning ...

If you were cooking meat as they did in your great-granddad's day, you'd start your fire by rubbing two sticks together. But because you're an impatient little pyromaniac, you can use a match. The only proviso here is that because no self-respecting man would resort to a gas barbecue, the following rules are written with hand-lit charcoal in mind ...

Step 1. Avoid self-lighting or additive-enhanced charcoal, unless you enjoy meat with the unmistakable taste of petroleum. Additive-free charcoal and natural wood lighters are far better bets and should be built into a nice neat pile in the middle of your barbecue. Bury three paraffin-free lighter cubes in triangle formation amongst them, light them and wait for the flames to spread.

Step 2. If you used lighter fluid to get things moving, you'll need to wait half an hour for their glues and additives to burn off. That's about as long as it takes for the flames to die down and reach a safe temperature to cook your meat over, so you can use the time to make any last-minute preparations to your meat, and perhaps to slip on your humorous 'tart-in-suspenders' apron.

Step 3. After thirty minutes the coals should be dusty white with a menacing red glow. This is a good sign. Cooking over raging flames may appear manly, but your meat will end up charred and undercooked, leaving you with a pair of comedy singed eyebrows and a bad case of the trots.

Step 4. Never poke and prod at the food with sharp implements as it cooks: it can damage the cells and set free the juices, which will leave your meat tasting as dry as an old cardboard boot. Instead, use tongs to turn your meat just once during cooking. If you're barbecuing under a lid, you're essentially roasting the meat so there's no need to turn it at all – it merely slows down the cooking process and irritates people.

Step 5. As a general rule, steak can be cooked as rare as you fancy (see below), but burgers, sausages and processed meats need to be cooked through until all sign of pink flesh is banished. Chicken is only safe to eat when the juices run clear and there's no sign of pink. Never eat charred meat as its cancer-causing chemicals are bad for you, unless the boffins have changed their view on this again.

Know your enemy
Bacteria love a barbecue even more than you do. They flourish in warm temperatures and double their number in twenty minutes, so avoid cross-contamination at all costs, unless you want to vomit until your ears bleed. Beef, particularly burgers, contains a high E. coli threat,

while with chicken it's the classic combination of salmonella and campylobacter, so there's potentially something for everyone. Make sure all meat is fully thawed before you begin cooking. Keep the raw and the cooked meat apart to prevent cross-contamination and use two sets of utensils, one for raw, one for cooked. Don't mix these or you might die.

Steak – the rule of thumb (or finger)

Cut the steak open to see if it's cooked and you'll drain it of all its tasty juices. The expert method of testing is to prod the meat as it cooks with your finger, using the following comparisons as your guide.

For rare: hold your hand out, fingers relaxed and naturally apart, then touch the area between thumb and forefinger with your other hand. Press the centre of a rare steak and it should feel the same.

For medium: stretch the fingers out further and prod the same flesh again. You've progressed to medium.

For well-done: clench the fist and prod once more. It should now feel tight. You can also feel the front of your nose, you should get the same firmness, unless you have the fat, flabby nose of a raging alcoholic.

How To ...
Take A Punch

That psychotic man at the bar has caught you eyeing up his pint, and now he wants to administer a sound beating. Blubbing like a child won't cut any ice with this fucker, so you'll have no choice but to defend yourself.

The following might just help you avoid a thorough kicking ...*

Your best bet is to try to out-manoeuvre him and pray someone steps in. Setting yourself up like a boxer would to give him less to aim at. Face him with your weaker arm to the front and raised 90 degrees at the elbow to protect your ribs, chest and face. Your punching arm should be furthest away from him, while your feet need to be firmly planted to give you a strong, solid base – but be ready to move quickly as he moves towards you.

As the fight unfolds:
If he throws a straight jab ...
Block his punch first with your arm on the same side as it's being

thrown. If it gets through, aim to meet it with your forehead. This may sound preposterous, but if he's going to land a punch on your pretty face you're far better off attempting to absorb the blow with the hardest part of your head, rather than your soft nose or vulnerable chin. Also, if he lands one with your head moving backwards, you'll feel the full force and stand more chance of being knocked off your feet. Tighten your neck muscles and jaw, and clench your teeth at the moment of impact. If your mouth is open and he lands a punch, the chances of it knocking you out and breaking your jaw increase.

Hit back with …
A hook. You can't dance around him all night, and hitting back is self-defence in this instance. So, protect your head with your left hand (provided you're right-handed) and by dropping your chin down to the middle of your left shoulder. As your right arm comes round his hands, turn your hand over so the palm is facing down and four knuckles land flush on the side of his head. Don't feel bad, you told him you didn't actually 'want some'.

If he throws an uppercut …
If he lands cleanly this could do serious damage to your chin or nose and dangerously whip your head back in the process, so try to block it with your arm and step to one side.

Hit back with …
A straight jab to the mush. Even though it's a straight punch, the fist should never land flat against his face or you risk doing your hand and wrist as much damage. Turn it so that it lands on his chin at a 45-degree angle.

Turn the fist slightly as you make contact. If you land your punch straight, you're likely to damage your hand.

If he throws a hook …
If this lands round the side of the head, it could do damage to your jaw and ear. Unless he's highly trained (in which case ignore these instructions and scarper), he should telegraph this particular shot, lurching back and giving you time to take the force of the blow on the forearm or elbow – imagine combing your hair as the punch is thrown because the action of blocking it with your arm is the same. You could also move in closer and allow his punch to fall behind your head, and, in theory, 'roll' underneath his punch. The latter takes clever timing and could result with you taking a knee to the face, which will smart.

Hit back with …
An uppercut. Lower your right shoulder to drop the right side of your body, keeping your left hand up to protect your chin. Rotate your hips forward and step into the

punch, bringing your shoulder forwards and up. The arm should stay close to the body throughout and the punch should land underneath his jaw, with the palm of your hand facing your chest as you finish. That'll teach him.

If he goes for the body ...
He could well kill you by landing a punch down below. If you see it coming, bring the elbows down while turning away from the shot. If you have no other option, move to the side slightly to take the shot on your obliques – the muscles on your sides which cover the ribs. This will still hurt, but at least you'll avoid damage to your vital organs. Never suck your stomach in if you see the shot coming, as you'll leave those vital organs exposed.

Hit back with ...
A hook (see above). It should be over by now, one way or another. If not, keep doing what you've been doing. He'll run out of puff soon. Probably.

*This skill assumes the assailant is up for a fair fight, one based very loosely on the Queensberry Rules. If you suspect he's carrying a pool ball in a sock, scream like a child and run.**
**Unless you happen to be really hard, in which case you don't need instructions.

Disclaimer: this entry covers the very basics of self-defence and is clearly no substitute for being taught pugilism properly, by experts. The publishers cannot condone fighting; it solves nothing and you may well end up on the wrong end of a sound thrashing. You have been warned.

How To ...
Deal With A Rather Nasty Cut

What started out as high jinks has escalated into horseplay and ended with an accident and claret everywhere. It's all very regrettable, but before the finger of blame can be pointed, it needs to stop gushing blood. Assess the situation. If the finger (or arm or whatever it is) is now hanging off by a thread, this is a job for a trained doctor, not you. If there's no threat of death by bleeding you can deal with it yourself by following these simple enough steps ...

Step 1. Take a clean cloth and press it gently onto the wound. This is mainly to stop the blood spurting out, but also to encourage the clotting process to begin.

Step 2. The heart pumps blood around the body, as you may already know. To reduce the supply to the wound, hold it above the level of the heart as soon as possible. For that reason, the victim should lie down on the floor, with their head lowered, feet raised and any tight clothing loosened, so much as taste and decency allows.

Step 3. Apply a dressing to the wound – which can be nothing more medicinal than a clean tea towel held in place by a bandage. Resist the urge to keep checking under the dressing to see if the blood has stopped bubbling; if anything, this will cause it to bleed more. And if the blood soaks through, simply apply another pad on top.

Step 4. Reassure the victim that it's not as bad as it feels, unless it is, in which case you should be almost at the hospital by now instead of reading this far down the page. If the cut still shows no sign of slowing, call an ambulance immediately. If the clotting has begun, run the wound under a tap, dry and apply a plaster or a light bandage. Nature can take care of the rest.

How to treat a really nasty burn

In this regrettable instance, someone has been left with a nasty burn. If it's any larger than a 50p piece, proceed directly to hospital. Provided it's not ridiculously deep, anything smaller can usually be treated very simply by the average man.

Place the burn under cold water for ten minutes to reduce pain and distress – this may also leave less of a mark on the skin.

To reduce the risk of infection, wrap the burn in cling film and allow the area to continue cooling. Left open to the air, the wound will be more uncomfortable and infection could end up with the limb falling off; although – yes – that is definitely a worse-case scenario, with no real evidence to support it.

How To ...
Gut A Fish

You've caught your tea using the Catch A Fish With A Piece Of String skill on page 90, now you'll need to remove its innards before you fry it in a pan, otherwise it won't taste at all pleasant. These instructions presume that you're simply looking for a nice big slab of fish for your tea, preferably one without the head staring back at you. (If you do want a fancy presentation fish, served up on a silver platter, see the box for instructions.) So, with a blunt instrument at the ready, follow these steps in this order ...

Step 1. If the fish is still wriggling about, hold it tight with one hand and crack it over the head, just behind the eyes, with a blunt instrument. It's kinder than gutting him alive and makes frying easier if he's not wriggling around and trying to escape. Clean off any blood under a tap before you begin the gutting process.

Step 2. Use a sharp knife to whip the pectoral fins off on either side.

Step 3. Using short strokes, run the knife's dull edge along the fish's flanks at a flat, 90-degree angle. If it runs smoothly the scales won't pose a problem and can stay. If there's resistance and the scales pop up, as they will with most salmon and trout, scrape them off until the fish is smooth.

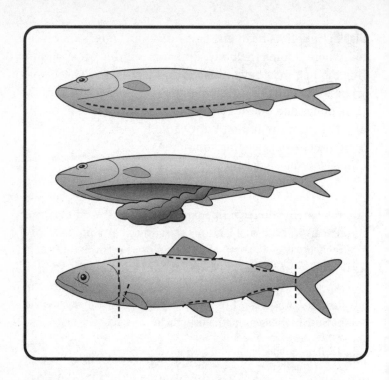

Step 4. The fun stuff starts here, providing your idea of fun is running a knife up through a dead fish's anus. Insert the point of the knife into the 'vent' (anus), and slice along the underside of the fish, past its belly, right the way up under the jaw and the gills (the flaps it once used for breathing, before you bludgeoned its brains out).

Step 5. Open the fish and remove its guts – use the knife to cut the sinewy bits and remove the no-longer-vital organs. Then take the tip of a knife and dig out the dark reddish-brown kidney line running along the backbone, which will make the fish taste muddy if you leave it in. Rinse the fish out thoroughly, just to be sure.

Step 6. Cut off its head just below the gills, then trim off the tail where it joins the body. Finish by cutting off any other fins the fish may have (this varies between the species) as well as the dorsal fin (the big one on the top) – it's full of little bones and doesn't taste nice. Cut either side of the fin and tug from the tail end outwards to pull the fin and its bones out. What remains should be cooked and eaten with chips (serving suggestion).

How to present posh fish

To impress guests at a swanky dinner party, you may prefer to present the fish as a whole (minus its guts, obviously) on a big silver platter. To do this, ignore steps 1, 2 and 6 – don't remove the scales, fins, gills or head, and when you slice into the fish's underside, cut up to and behind the gills on either side until the head is held on only by the backbone. Serve to gasps of amazement, perhaps ditching greasy chips and having some nice new potatoes and a smattering of vegetables instead.

How To...
Throw A Boomerang

At first glance this could have been held back for the follow-up publication to his book: *Pointless Skills*. However, delve a little deeper and you'll discover that a boomerang can be used as a weapon for hunting and fighting, an impromptu percussion instrument and, apparently, as a fire starter. So for any man who ever needs to fight a pig to the death, play a celebratory tune on its trotters and then cook it to a crisp over a raging fire, the boomerang is essential.

Should you also wish to throw the boomerang away and watch it return for no other reason than it might be mildly entertaining, well, this magic stick can do that too ...

Step 1. Find yourself an open space, but before you set up, check there are no romping toddlers, ice sculptures or tradesmen carrying a large pane of glass back and forth across your path. If the coast is clear, grip the boomerang with the flat side to the palm, with the (near) end sitting around the middle of the palm, being supported by the thumb and first two fingers. The tip of the boomerang should then rest on the top of your third finger.

Step 2. Raise the wood above your shoulder and only ever throw it straight forward in an upright position (see fig. 1). If you're right-handed, angle the boomerang approximately 10 degrees to the right (10 degrees to the left for the left-handed minority). The angle at which you throw the boomerang depends on strength of the wind (fig. 2). If it's blowing hard, angle the boomerang a little more inwards, if it's calm, angle it a little further outwards. Trial and error will tell you how far to go – but never throw it vertically upright.

Step 3. Resist the temptation to throw the boomerang up in the air – it will climb naturally, as if by magic – so aim no more than 20 degrees above the horizon. Finally, never throw from a standing position, with your feet just plonked side by side. If you're right-handed, make sure your left foot is stepping forward as you throw (and vice versa for lefties), then apply a flick of your wrist to give it as much spin as possible as it leaves your hand. Thanks to advanced physics too tedious and indeed complex to go into here, when you let go the boomerang should 'right' itself as it commences its turn and return to you spinning in the horizontal position. But what if … oh buggery … it's arcing straight back for your head!

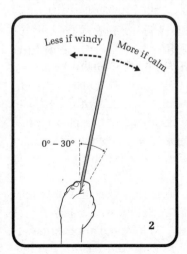

Less if windy · More if calm

0° – 30°

2

3

Step 4. Fear not. Simply follow its path and prepare yourself to catch it at the side of your body by clasping it in the palms of both hands (fig. 3) as it passes by. Unless you enjoy the taste of blood and broken teeth, never attempt to catch the boomerang at face level, and only attempt to catch it one-handed if you're a flash twat.

A few words of warning

1. Throwing a boomerang straight into a strong wind is asking for trouble, especially if it blows straight back towards your delicate face. Anything over 5 mph is considered to be 'too strong'. If in doubt, lick your finger, raise it to the wind and pull a face that suggests you're assessing the conditions. After an age, shake your head and suggest opening the picnic eggs instead.

2. Always wait until the sky is clear before throwing. Kites, low-flying aircraft, hovering birds of prey and other boomerangs clogging up the airways will all conspire to bugger up your attempt.

3. Keep your eye on the boomerang throughout the throw. If it arcs back towards you, prepare to catch safely (see main copy, and also warning no. 4 below). If it flies off and shows no sign of returning, follow its path to where it finally rests or risk losing your precious stick for ever.

4. If the boomerang is arcing back towards you, but appears to have picked up too much speed as it hones in on your head, turn your back on it, bend over and protect your skull with your arms. Otherwise it may take your head clean off.

Warning: this advice is only valid for boomerangs designed to be thrown rather than used as over-priced decorative trinkets bought by gullible tourists, which aren't designed to be thrown.

How To ...
Pull A Tooth

The swinging door method was very popular in the days of black-and-white films, when brave men were driven to the edge of insanity by a throbbing tooth. You could always pull a rotten tooth out using pliers, of course, but that's far less impressive than employing the swinging door method. All you'll need is a line of string, a door and a high pain threshold ...

Open wide!

The line needs to be fine enough to tie first round your chosen tooth, then round the door knob, but robust enough not to snap when the door is slammed shut.

Said door should be heavy enough to provide the force needed to yank the tooth clean out.

Work out how far away you'll need to stand so that when the door shuts the line becomes taut, then anaesthetize the pain you're about to feel with strong booze. Plant both feet firmly on the ground and swing the door hard towards its fra ... eh? What's this?

Ah, it says here that under no circumstances whatsoever should any man (or woman) ever attempt to pull his own tooth, and particularly not using the irresponsible Line-Of-String-And-Swinging-Door Technique.

Apparently, even if the tooth is loose, the bone holding it in place will still be strong. By pulling it out, either using the door or a pair of pliers, you'll almost certainly break off the top of the tooth, spread the infection, possibly break your jaw and maybe end up with a life-threatening abscess, having first gone into shock due to the trauma of it all. If you're unable to staunch the blood loss, you're likely to need transfusions, unless you die first.

Alternatively ...

The alternative approach, of course, is to contact a dentist in your neighbourhood and make an emergency appointment. They'll either operate or prescribe drugs to numb the pain, and by the time the tooth has been taken care of you should still have full use of your mouth.

How To...
Pull Off A Card Trick

Every man should know just one card trick so as to keep innocent children and gullible women entertained. Mastering any more than one 'sleight of hand' marks you down as an eccentric loner with too much time on his hands. Learning 'just one more' is probably how it started for that oddball Blaine.

So, if you're only going to learn one trick, make it one of the easiest in the book: the Card In The Wallet trick. You'll allow your victim to pick a card from the pack, any card at all. Then, through a combination of cunning chicanery and barefaced deceit, you'll pull the very same card they plucked from the deck out of your wallet.

The preparation

In case you hadn't guessed, you'll need two decks of cards, which will give you two of the same card. Any card will suffice, but for the purpose of this example we'll use the Jack of Diamonds.

Put one of these Diamond-Jacks in your wallet. Now, add a small square of double-sided tape on the underside of the wallet and put it away in your pocket. Put the other Jack on the top of the deck and prepare to make magic happen.

The trick

Pull the wallet out, making certain the tape is hidden from

view, and announce that inside lies a miracle – or some other such magic-based hocus pocus. Be warned though, that if anyone sees the tape, your trick is well and truly buggered and you'll look like the charlatan you are.

But they haven't seen the tape, so fan the cards out towards them and ask them to remove any card from anywhere in the deck* – but not to look at it. Take the card from them and put it face down on top of the deck.

Now bring in more smoke and mirrors. In order to distract your prey, stare into their eyes and waffle on once more about miracles happening, and how you will soon reveal to them the card they chose: at the same time, and without being observed (and that bit's very important), place the wallet (tape-side down) on top of the deck. Press down firmly on it so that now, as you pick the wallet back up, the tape picks up the victim's card and leaves the Jack of Diamonds back on top of the deck.

Now, announce that your victim must turn over the card they'd picked. As they do so, and the Jack is revealed, they'll believe this to be the card they freely chose.

Finally, open your wallet and whip out the stashed second Jack (keeping the underside of the wallet – and the card stuck there – well and truly concealed). Now, unless something's gone badly wrong, you should have hoodwinked the fop. Announce 'that's magic!' in a squeaky voice, keeping to yourself that it's really nothing more than low-level deceit.

*If the victim selects the card on top of the pile, panic not. Simply proceed as normal, but make certain you skip the sticky tape procedure at the end.

How To...
Whistle Through Your Fingers

The shrill toot of the magical finger whistle is not only an essential skill for any dog fans reading, it's also good for when ... erm, if you need to ... er ... Actually, summoning dogs is about all it is good for, but one toot and that mutt will know who's in charge.

The technique
Step 1. Form a 'U' or 'V' shape with your fingers by loosely touching the ends of your bent index finger and thumb.

Step 2. Rest your fingers (if you're using your right hand, the thumb should be to the right) on your lower teeth.

Step 3. The tips of your fingers should be resting against the bottom front part of your tongue, and pushing it back into your mouth so it rests just behind your bottom row of teeth.

Step 4. Press your lips down against your fingers, which form the 'U' or 'V' into which you must blow. The sound is created by your upper teeth and tongue forcing air on to the lower lip and teeth. Apparently.

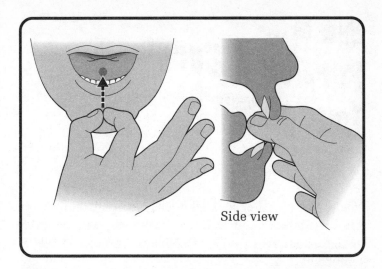

Side view

Step 5. As you blow, you may initially find that it's nothing more than a pitiful wheezing noise which leaves your fingers covered in spittle. Keep practising and fine-tuning the position of the fingers, and you should soon possess a shrill toot, plus a dozen dogs by your side.

How To ...
Survive A Car
Emergency

You're just plodding along the road, as usual, well within the speed limit and dutifully respecting all the other vehicles on the road, when ... ah balls ... we appear to have a problem ...

Your tyre blows

It's very easy to say this from here, but do try not to panic. If the tyre blows, particularly a front tyre, your car will try to take you in a different direction – towards the damaged wheel.

The worst thing you could ever do is jump on the brake pedal in a blind panic. You'll end up with a tattooed truck driver ploughing straight up your arse, or worse. If there is worse. And there probably isn't.

Instead of panicking, gently ease off the gas, keeping your hands firmly clamped on the wheel in the '10 to 2' position. As you ease off, try to remember where the hazard warning light switch is and flick it on, then go down through the gears to slow the car as you move it safely to the side of the road.

Once you've slowed to a safe speed, apply the brake gently, bring the car to a halt and gulp loudly.

The engine fails!

Why and how the engine's failed is not really the most pressing issue at this moment in time, as it's all very technical. Yes, you're right, I don't pretend to have the first clue, but all you really need to know is how to react. Luckily, this one's fairly simple: put the car into neutral, signal your intentions and brake gently. Without the engine's assistance braking and steering takes more effort, but compared to a blowout this is a doddle. Reduce speed until you can pull off the road safely. Stop. Switch ignition off. Switch on hazard warning lights and get out. Call breakdown-recovery service. Wait an age. Call again and ask what's taking so long. Wait some more. Prepare to pay through the nose.

You're starting to skid!!

The road is snowy, icy or just wet, and without warning your car starts to skid. The most unexpected skids occur on wet roads, with what's known as aquaplaning. When this happens, a layer of water between the tyres and the road surface reduces the tyres' friction and, therefore, their grip. That's the technical stuff over, here's how to save the situation.

Resist the natural urge to hit the brakes – you'll be face first in a ditch before you can mutter 'Oh buggery.' Instead, depress the clutch, ease off the accelerator and simply (and smoothly) steer into the direction of the skid until you've regained control of the car.

In wintery conditions, preparation is often the key. If snow has fallen or there's a decent chance of ice being on the roads, you'll be wearing comfortable footwear at the wheel rather than snow-clad boots, to give you greater control on the pedals. You'll also be driving at a much slower, safe speed, avoiding any sudden jerky movements and reducing your rate of travel to a pensioner plod as you approach any bends.

You'll have checked the pressure and tread depth of your tyres before venturing out (3 mm tread is OK, less than 2 mm is asking for trouble), and obviously you'll have packed a shovel in the boot in case you get snowed under, and a nice flask of soup. Diligent preparation is the mark of a ball-ache, but at least you'll reach your destination in one piece and with the warm glow of satisfaction that only a good cream of tomato can give.

The effing accelerator's only gone and jammed!!!

If this happens, you can consider yourself very unlucky indeed. But there's no time to mope about as you'll need to have your wits about you if you're to avoid a major incident. Fortunately, if you have your head screwed on, it's not too difficult to come to a safe stop.

Flick the gears into neutral, apply the brakes gently, indicate and steer on to the side of the road. Only then, when the car's stationary, should you turn the ignition off. Try turning it off in a blind panic while you're driving (in the not unreasonable supposition it will cut the engine) and you may find the steering locks, making an already tricky job a whole lot harder. Once the car has stopped safely, turn the ignition off as soon as humanly possible, otherwise you'll inflict serious damage on your engine (which is probably at this point revving itself hoarse, given the car's still in neutral). Switch on those hazard lights and call the breakdown-recovery people. By now you should have their number on speed-dial.

And the brakes have failed!!!!

Oh fuck, this one's not good. Think fast, act sharp and keep your eyes on the road at all times. Firstly, try pumping the brake pedal, and if you're very lucky, the pressure may come back long enough to enable you to stop safely.

If it doesn't, slowly apply the handbrake, drop down into a lower gear and the added drag should slow the car down and allow you to pull over at a safe stopping point. Never try this on a corner, however, as the car could spin out of control. The key with this skill is to act as quickly, but calmly, as possible. Survive this and you've escaped every car-based emergency imaginable. Surely.

Ah balls, to top it all, now the bonnet has flown open!!!!!

You'd have to laugh, were it not for the fact you can't see that you're about to wrap your car around a tree. The worst reaction, as ever, is to slam the brakes on hard – the vehicles behind will plough straight into you. A better bet would be to begin to slow gently and look to see if the road ahead is visible in the gap between the dashboard and the bonnet. If not, you'll need to do the Dog Manoeuvre and stick your head out of the window to see what's ahead of you, with the slobbery tongue sticking out an optional extra. Slow down smoothly, pull off to the side of the road and think hard about buying a more reliable car.

How To ...
Eat Lobster

You've bought, caught or ordered a nice big lobster for your tea, and he's currently being boiled alive on the stove over there. The only problem is that you're somewhat inexperienced when it comes to fine dining and you've never eaten the king of crustaceans before. You wouldn't know a telson from a tomalley, nor which bit to snap and what you should suck. Luckily, here's a short cut. Allow him to cool after cooking, prod him with your fork to make sure he's dead, then attack in the following order ...

Step 1. Hold the back and twist off the legs. They contain minuscule morsels which can be scraped or sucked straight out like a fishy straw.

Step 2. Break off the claws by twisting them at the joints. Bend the thumby claw back to separate it from the crusher and scrape out the meat inside the shell. Use a nutcracker or heavy knife to break the crusher claw and plunder the meat inside.

Step 3. Twist the tail into two parts, then break off the tail flippers (which contain the aforementioned telson) and extract what little meat they contain. The main piece contains the lobster's tastiest meat. Push the tail meat out and on to your plate in one piece, peeling off and discarding the dirty black vein that runs the length of this section.

Step 4. Tackling the main body is generally left to the intrepid. Grip it at the hole left where you removed the tail and pull the shell away from the body. Inside you'll find the gills, the circulation system and the green digestive gland (that tomalley thing). If it's a female lobster, there may also be unfertilized eggs. The tomalley and the eggs are both edible if you're not fussy and still hungry.

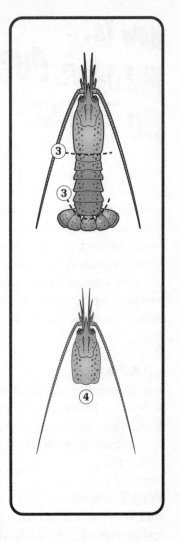

Step 5. Even if you'll eat anything and are still peckish after steps 1 to 4, avoid the antennae, antennules and the big beak at all costs. They're inedible and would give you indigestion and terrible wind.

How To...
Mend A Puncture
On A Bike

The sound of hissing is the dirty great thorn stuck fast in your bicycle tyre. It will soon be joined by the sound of steam billowing angrily from your ears when you realize your bike-based fun is at an end.

So, instead of bunny-hopping about the park like a small boy sky-high on E-numbers, you now have no choice but to carry the thing home in a childlike huff and set about fixing the puncture ...

You'll need:
- 1 puncture-repair kit or spare inner tube
- 2 tyre levers, available from all good bike shops
- 1 spanner to release the wheel (unless it's a quick-release model)
- 1 pump

Ready to operate
Step 1. Flip the bike on its head and remove the nut or the quick-release lever to take off the wheel. Use the tyre levers to prise the tyre from the rim – section by section, until the tyre and inner tube come free.

Step 2. Run your mitts round the inside of the tyre to check for the nail or thorn or whatever it was wot burst your tyre. Remove the offending object and study it at close quarters for a few moments, mutter a dark expletive, then cast it aside while you check the rest of the tyre to make sure there are no other pointy things left in there.

Step 3. Find the hole in the inner tube either by pumping it up or holding it under water – the bubbles should give it away. Mark it with a pen or chalk, ideally using a Union Jack-style cross over the hole. Taking the emery paper from your puncture-repair kit, scuff the area around the hole until the middle of the cross is erased completely – this will make it easier to secure the glue to the inner tube. And now, even though the centre of the cross has been scuffed away, the eight lines of the Union Jack should still point you to the centre (and therefore the hole).

Step 4. Spread a penny-sized blob of glue evenly around the hole, making sure it's bigger than the puncture-repair-kit patch. Let it dry until it feels tacky, then apply a small blob of glue to the underside of the patch, place the patch over the hole and push it down firmly for at least a minute. Wait for a couple of minutes more before carefully peeling off the backing.

Step 5. Check the inside edge of the outer tyre again to make sure there are no sharp pointy bits lurking, then pump just enough air into the inner tube to give it a nice wheel-shaped shape; don't forget to push the valve stem through the rim's hole. While sniggering childishly at that previous phrase, make sure the valve fits through comfortably to avoid any later complications. Now push the tube into the rim all the way round, making sure it's the right way round and not twisted.

Step 6. Work the outer tyre back over the wheel rim, using tyre levers or fingers to make sure it's in all the way round. Pump more air in to check the tube isn't caught between the rim and the tyre. Reattach the wheel and pump it up fully.

Step 7. Realize that you could have avoided steps 1 to 6 altogether by paying a man in the bike shop £10 to do it for you. Then accept that it wouldn't have made much of an entry. What's that you say? Eh? Oh. Yes, fair point.

How To...
Cook The Fish You Caught On Page 90
(And Gutted On Page 177)

Unless you're a Japanese lad, you'll want to cook your fish before you eat him. (If you are a Japanese lad, please ignore this entry and turn over – raw fish holds no fear for you.)

We're assuming you're still stuck out in the wilderness, living on your wits and by now sporting a large straggly beard that's starting to smell slightly off. Unfortunately, because you forgot to bring salt, pepper, garlic butter and your hand-crafted revolving spice rack, it's plain fish for tea again, cooked over a crackling fire with only the flies for company.

Fish spoils soon after death, particularly when it's hot and humid. Eat a rotten fish and as revenge for killing him and whipping out his guts expect vomiting, paralysis and a terrible case of the trots. So clearly you'll need to act fast.

Having gutted him you could, in theory, cook your fish over the hot coals on a simple fire, but for that you'd need to cook it in thick aluminium foil, which you may not have, or banana leaves, if you're slumming it in a Latin American forest. If you have the wherewithal, simply wait for the flames to die down and for the coals to turn white and smoldering before shoving the fish on to cook. Give him ten minutes per 2.5 cm of thickness, and turn halfway through. Unwrap and eat, probably with your fingers.

Alternatively ...

For the man with no foil or thick leaves to hand, your best bet is to impale Mr Fish on a clean stick, make several large slashes across his skin to ensure the flesh cooks more evenly throughout, and hold him over the hot coals for a few minutes, taking care not to burn him to a tasteless crisp. To check that he's cooked, cut into the back of the fish and the flesh next to the bone should be opaque, not translucent. When he's done, eat him.

How To ...
Mix A Killer Cocktail

For those occasions when a pint of Olde Scrote and a white wine spritzer doesn't quite seem appropriate ...

For Her ... a Cosmopolitan
The one those women drink in that programme.

Ingredients
Citrus vodka
Cointreau (or triple sec)
Fresh lime juice
Cranberry juice
Ice cubes
25ml spirit measure
Cocktail shaker
Cocktail glass
Strainer
One fresh orange
Cigarette lighter

Instructions
1. Pour 1 measure citrus vodka, 1/2 measure of Cointreau, 1 measure fresh lime juice and 1 measure cranberry juice into cocktail shaker. Fill with ice and shake, having put the top on first.

2. Strain contents into a cocktail glass.

3. Cut a small piece of orange zest, and warm the skin side with the cigarette lighter. Hold the orange zest over the centre of the drink and squeeze over the flame – oil from the orange zest should ignite and create a bright yellow flame. Wipe the rim of the glass with the orange zest and drop into the glass. Serve.

For Him ... a dry Martini
The king of all cocktails.

Ingredients
Dry vermouth
Gin or vodka (optional)
Ice cubes
Cocktail glass
Mixing glass
25ml spirit measure
Long-bar spoon
Strainer
Cocktail olives
Cocktail sticks (optional)
One fresh lemon

Instructions
1. Put the ice cubes into a cocktail glass and cover with cold water. This will chill the glass nicely.

2. Fill the mixing glass with ice and pour in a little dry vermouth. Stir for several seconds with the bar spoon and then strain off the vermouth and excess water. This way the ice gets coated with vermouth and the mixing glass gets chilled.

3. Add 3 measures of gin or vodka into the mixing glass over the remaining ice and stir well.

4. Empty the chilled water from the cocktail glass and strain in the gin or vodka.

5. Garnish with either 3 cocktail olives on a stick or use a knife to cut a little piece of lemon zest and squeeze the oil from the lemon zest on top of the drink.

6. Make a lemon twist by cutting a strip of peel into a quarter-inch-thick strip and twist like a corkscrew. Wipe the rim of the glass with it and drop it into the Martini. Now guzzle the glass dry.

How To ...
Fix A Dripping Tap

A dripping tap can test the patience of any man. Water experts claim even a slight drip can drain 140 litres of water a week, which is a good 28 buckets. Extrapolate that over three years and you'd have enough water to fill your own private boating lake with adjoining water park.

Obviously a dripping tap costs you money, but it can also stain your sink or bath and deprive you of sleep in the darkest hours with that incessant drip, drip, effing drip. Oh Christ, when will it ever stop? When you bother to replace the washer (available for a few pence from all DIY stores), because that's all it normally takes ...

Before you begin, however, avoid being sprayed in hapless comedy fashion by turning the water supply off. The stop valve responsible for this is normally located close to where the water pipe enters the building. It's often, but not always, under the sink – locate it in advance before you need it in an emergency.

Turn on the sink tap to remove any water lurking in the pipes. When it runs dry turn it off and put the plug in to prevent those small fiddly parts you will inevitably drop from falling down the plug hole.

For the common, conventional tap (fig. 1), you'll need to carefully remove the top by unscrewing the little nut by hand or with a spanner. If it's a more modern tap (fig.2),

Washer

Fig. 1   Fig. 2

the screw will be concealed under the hot and cold indicators.

If you unscrew the nut using a spanner, shove a cloth underneath to avoid scratching your nice shiny tap, and when undoing the hexagonal nut, hold the tap to prevent it rotating and buggering up your sink or bath.

Taps vary and the washer will either be in the headgear you've just removed or on the valve seating (the shelf on which the washer sits) still attached to the tap. It may also be held in place by a small retaining nut, which will need unscrewing. The old washer will look like the new washer, only older and much shabbier.

Prise it off and attach the new one, then reverse the instructions above to screw the headgear back on to the tap, taking care not to over-tighten.

Turn the water supply back on and if the dripping's stopped, this entry is finished for you. Congratulations.

If it's still as bad as before, the valve seating may be worn or coated with limescale. Invest in a valve-seat grinder (also available from DIY stores), push the end into the tap and twist to clean the metal work and provide a flat, flush surface for the washer to sit on.

Reassemble as above, and if the drip still continues, lose your temper before calling a proper plumber who can end this sorry charade once and for all. Ah well, at least you tried.

How To ...
Change A Tyre

That funny rumbling noise and the overall lopsided feel to the car suggests one of your tyres has a flat. This can't be ignored by turning up the radio, so you'll have to replace it with the spare. Here's what to do ...

Spare change

To minimize the damage to the wheel, slow down to biddy pace (5 mph should do) and pull off to a safe place. (To minimize possible damage to yourself, check you've not pulled over near any stick-wielding ne'er-do-wells.)

Turn off the engine, make sure the hazard lights are on and apply the handbrake – if it's a manual car, put it in reverse. If automatic, select 'P' for 'park'.

Remove luggage and passengers to lighten the load, and put down one of those warning-triangle things, if you're one of the few people who actually owns one. This will discourage truck drivers from ploughing into you, provided they haven't dropped off after thirty-seven straight hours at the wheel. If that happens, the triangle won't save you.

Now check to find your spare tyre (it's normally in the boot and needs to be fully inflated) and the essential tools you will need – a wheel brace and jack, plus your car's handbook. Without these you can't proceed and will need to call for help or extend your thumb the towards slow lane. If you have all the bits, you're all set ...

The start

Step 1. First, you need to remove the wheel trim (aka the hubcap), which is the plastic disk that covers the centre of the wheel – unless you have alloy wheels, in which case this instruction doesn't apply and you've just wasted seven seconds you'll never get back. Prise it off with your fingers or with the end of the wheel brace. This is much easier when the car's still grounded, so take the brace and give the wheel nuts just a half-turn anticlockwise. To keep the wheel stable and balanced, unscrew them diagonally (unscrew one, then the one diagonally opposite to it, and try to keep up). If the nuts are particularly stiff, either coat them with a little oil and leave for a few minutes, or hold one end of the wrench with your hand and step on the other end with your clumpy great foot.

Step 2. Your handbook should suggest the safest, sturdiest lifting point on the car to place the jack. If the jack point is anything less than perfectly secure then you, shabby fool, are asking for trouble – jacks can easily slip, even on flat surfaces.

When the jack is in place, insert the handle and slowly turn to raise the car. You'll need to jack it just high enough for the damaged wheel to still be touching the ground, but far enough for the spare tyre to slide flat under the car's body. If the car does slip off the jack the tyre will at least cushion the blow. Keep jacking up until the flat tyre is just clear of the road, then continue to unscrew the nuts in diagonal pairs and remove them. Place them in your pocket and keep them safe. In your pocket.

Step 3. Remove the wheel, which will be heavy and coated in a combination of oil, dirt and probably some dead vermin or other. Place it under the raised edge of the car for cushioning (having obviously removed the spare tyre from there first). Stick the good tyre onto the hub, the right way round, and fit the nuts on in diagonal formation again, tightening with your fingers for now. The nuts, yes. Didn't you put them in your pocket? ...

Use the jack to lower the car until the tyre just touches the ground, then tighten the nuts properly and refit the wheel trim.

The end

Shove the damaged tyre in the boot, lower the car fully and remove the jack. Refill the car with bags and people, mirror, signal and manoeuvre on your way.

Ditch the doughnuts

If your spare is what those in the trade call a 'spacesaver' or 'doughnut', it's a temporary tyre designed only to get you to the nearest garage, where an oily mechanic will replace it with a sturdier model. Never exceed 40 mph on a temporary tyre – and replace the damaged tyre asap.

And with your safety in mind, never, ever attempt to change a wheel on the hard shoulder of a motorway – a lorry could very easily clip your head off. Put your hazard lights on, call the breakdown patrol men and stand a safe distance (10 metres or so) behind the car and away from the road.

How To...
Buy Her A Present
She Might Actually
Like For Once

How would I know? I've never even met her. However, if she's anything like most women then you'd do well to listen to her a bit more, and try to retain at least some of the information she tells you. Pay particular attention in the run-up to birthdays and Christmas when she's guaranteed to drop hints.

However, if you've had your fingers in your ears for the last few months and have been totally oblivious to all her pointers, you'll need to do some homework. The first sensible thing to do is to ask her best mate, who will normally know exactly what to suggest and will be flattered to be consulted (and will of course tell your lady friend all about how sweetly hopeless you were afterwards. For some reason, they like that kind of thing.) Don't ask her mum, however, unless you actively want your future mother-in-law to think you are an unimaginative, unromantic, lazy tit. It's also worth having a surreptitious flick through the latest issue of your lady's favourite magazine, which will usually give you a few clues as to what's 'in' and 'out' this month, not to mention a better understanding of acceptable penis dimensions.

Still stuck for ideas? Sadly, there are no one-size-fits-all rules where women are concerned; they're a complicated breed. However, exhaustive studies have revealed that the following gifts tick most boxes:

- Anything you've put a bit of thought and effort into – which rules out almost everything you can buy from the petrol station the night before her big day. Think girly: an album of special photos, perhaps, even if most of the snaps show her and her friends boggle-eyed on booze in a karaoke bar. An old-fashioned mix tape of her favourite songs, or some hard-to-find, cherished book from her childhood will also score highly.

- A home-made 'voucher' of some kind – whether it's for a no-expenses-spared dinner for two followed by a night in a trendy boutique hotel or a simple 'I promise to babysit, shop, clean, cook, wash up and wait on you for a whole weekend so you can put your feet up.' Consider it a role reversal, for she certainly will.

- Any luxury item she would never normally justify spunking a large bundle of notes on – a cashmere jumper (or scarf, if you're skint, you tight fecker), a hand-stitched, leather-bound notebook, or even a selection of really good-quality chocolates from a proper chocolatier (go for an over-priced Belgian box, rather than Cadbury's).

- An unusual, unexpected day out – a day at the races, a picnic by the sea, a trip up the river in a smart boat, a night at the opera, an afternoon at a posh spa, that kind of thing. Expect to be marked down for the beer garden at the Dog and Ferret.

- Perfume, jewellery, flowers and lingerie are always popular, but can be a bugger to get right. With your lady's smalls, make sure you get the size, even if it means snooping through her underwear drawer on the sly. Never allow her to catch you snooping through her underwear drawer, of course, and remember you're buying said smalls for her, not you. If it looks like a frilly cheese wire, its probably not been designed with her comfort in mind.

And buying her a present when it's not an 'occasion' wouldn't hurt either – the element of surprise and all that.

How To...
Clean The Windows Like A Pro

If you can no longer see the postman approaching due to a build-up of grime and bird dirt, it's probably about time to give the windows a quick once over. For the most professional finish, call a window cleaner with a good reputation in the area. For the next best thing at a fraction of the cost, do it yourself. Experts recommend you wash them twice a year at the very least, which doesn't sound unreasonable.

You'll need:
- One squeegee – the wide-headed tool with the smooth rubber blade which removes water without leaving dirty streaks. Available from all good DIY stores.
- A sponge – or for a more professional approach, a T-bar washer with a mop head. It's shaped like the letter 'T' and has a big straggly mop on top. Also available from all good DIY stores.
- A bucket of cold water with a hearty glug of washing-up liquid – warm water is more likely to streak.
- A nice little chamois leather.

Before you begin

Assess the weather: if it's sunny and the windows are hot, they'll dry too fast and streak, which you may have gathered by now is the worst thing that can happen in a window-cleaner's world (apart from falling off a ladder or through the pane). If it is warm and sunny, go and sit in the back garden and come back when it's cloudy, dry and miserable.

Clean

It's a cloudy, dry, miserable day, so begin by removing any loose debris on or around the window. Use the mop head on the T-bar thing or your sponge and wash down the windowsills and frames. If you leave the sills and frames until after the window, you'll almost certainly splash water down your newly-cleaned, streak-free pane, and then you'll have to start again.

Wash

Soak your T-bar thing with just enough soapy water to cover the pane – you don't need to saturate it. Put your back into it to remove those stubborn stains, especially the grime you've allowed to build up in the corners of the frame. The professionals swear by a razor blade to scrape off any heavy-duty bird dirt more easily, though the blade has to be wet or you'll scratch the glass.

Wipe

Before you squeegee the window, wet the blade with a damp cloth so that it doesn't 'skip' across the surface of the glass. Place the squeegee in the top left corner of the window, so the blade sits vertically and against the window edge.

Press it firmly and pull across the window in one sweeping movement. Wipe the squeegee dry with a paper towel (to avoid creating streaks), and then repeat on the section below, overlapping slightly so you cover the entire pane.

Pull, wipe clean, move down. Repeat the process until finally you reach the bottom, and wipe away any water at the base of the window frame with a damp chamois leather – it soaks up water without leaving – see if you can finish that sentence yourself, reader ...

A fine finish

According to people who wash their windows more often and thoroughly than you and I, a supreme finish can be achieved by scrunching up a sheet or two of old newspaper and polishing the now-clean glass. Others claim this'll leave you with ink down your nice clean windows.

Equally contentious is the suggestion that adding vinegar to your cleaning solution will guarantee a streak-free clean. Some say it works, others say it's cobblers.

Falling down

There are many heroic and manly ways to meet your maker, but falling off a ladder with a squeegee in your hand is not one of them. If you need to reach just that little bit higher, buy a squeegee extender pole thing.

If you have to use a ladder, make sure it's angled safely (never more than 75 degrees), planted on stable ground and that you never overreach, otherwise you'll be left hanging off the guttering or dead on the ground below. And nobody wants that. Or so you'd like to think ...

How To ...
Dance

To be more exact, that should read How To ... Dance Without Looking And Feeling Like A Club-Footed Tosser, or that tragic uncle who bounds around the floor at weddings looking like that bloke from Joy Division. Tragically, at some point in your life you'll be forced into a situation where you have to dance. When that happens, you'll either have to lock yourself in the toilet or wish you'd paid closer attention to this page ...

Some basic rules

1. Almost all men are shit dancers. Some know how to cover up their natural lack of rhythm better than you do, the rest don't care.

2. Most men who dance are making it up as they go along. They don't have an elaborate choreographed dance routine worked out. Watch them (on the sly) for more than six seconds and that much will become clear.

3. Most men who dance know that confidence goes a long way. Professional dancers refer to it as 'attitude': the ability to make others believe you know what you're doing.

4. Any man who has a basic move will elevate himself above the dance-floor shufflers. They will think you have natural rhythm, you will know that you've simply followed The Most Basic Dance Move Ever Devised ...

The most basic dance move ever devised ...

Study any dance move closely enough and you'll find an element of the Step-Touch. So that's what you're learning today, and when you read how simple it is you'll be wondering if you can have your money back for this entry.

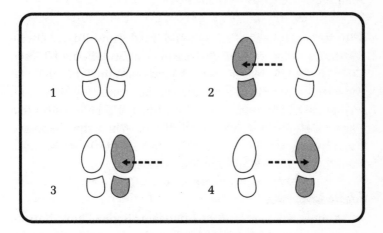

1. Stand with your legs a comfortable distance apart. No, only you can determine 'comfortable'.

2. Listen to the track and step one leg to the side *on the beat*.

3. Keeping 'on beat', bring the other leg over so that you're back in your starting position, albeit to the side of where you began.

4. On the next beat, repeat the move to the other side, and continue to repeat on alternative sides for the rest of the song.

5. There is no 5, that's really all there is to it.

The beauty of the Step-Touch is that the technique remains the same whether you go left or right, backwards or forwards. All you really need to remember is to step on the beat, otherwise you'll look foolish.

Bring in the arms ...

Bear in mind that if you're only moving your feet you're doing nothing more than a glorified shuffle. Introduce the arms and you progress to dancing proper. Arm action makes everything more expressive – which is where most men make tail ends of themselves.

The key is to keep both arms tight and project confidence, maybe even something approaching a jaunty swagger. Never let your arms hang down limply like you don't know what you're meant to do with them – you now know that's not the point.

Start with the most basic arm move: a glorified jogging motion where they just appear to bounce up and down. You're right, it's a bit shit, but it looks passable as long as you're still moving in time to the beat.

From there, build in something slightly more impressive. As you move your foot to the right, move your arms and point your right index finger that way, or roll your fists over each other in that direction. When you step onto the left foot, do the same in that direction.

Now, if you're confident enough with all that, you may as well pull out the classic 70s disco arm move. This time, as you step to the left, on the beat, push your left arm up high and point. Step back to the right and repeat on that side with your right arm and hand. Any dance is a statement, and your 70s disco move screams: 'I'm out of my depth, and I don't have any idea how to stop!'

So, that just about covers the most basic of basics. From here, both the legs and arms begin to move in ever more complex ways, and before you know it you're spinning on your head, which now sports an ill-advised afro. So yes, it's probably best we leave it at that for now.

How To ...
Dance Properly, Like A Dandy

For the more refined gentleman who considers himself above chasing strumpets across sleazy nite-spot floors using a shabby touch-step dance routine, it may be worth considering learning to dance like a dandy.

Ballroom dancing has been around in various forms for an age. It used to be an upper-class pursuit, while the commoners were forced to content themselves with folk dancing and fighting bears. Nowadays, class doesn't count for much. Indeed the most prestigious international dance event is held annually in Blackpool, and many of the more accomplished ballroom artistes are brassy commoners dripped in fake tan and cheap jewellery.

If you were to ask them to recommend one dance move for the novice to learn, they'd probably suggest the Swing Boogie, Disco Fox or Carolina Shag. But because we're looking to start with the basics and need to keep things simple, you might be better off mastering the basics of the waltz – a timeless classic taken from the German word *walzen*, meaning to glide. You're a man, so you should lead and she should follow. It turns out the basics are a doddle ...

The Waltz

Face your partner and place your right hand on their waist, a little towards the back. Your left arm should be held out to the left, elbow bent and your palm raised about shoulder height to facing her. Her right hand should grasp your left loosely, her left hand should rest on your right shoulder, her elbow bent rather than fully outstretched. Now you're set, tell her to hang on, wait for the beat and follow these steps.

Dance gracefully on the tips of your toes. Look straight ahead, which should be into her eyes or eye, if she's one of those women who wears a patch. The experts suggest you count 'one, two, three', 'one, two, three' as you waltz, placing emphasis and moving off on the 'one' count.

On the first beat ('one'), step forward with your left foot, gliding as gracefully as possible. She should mirror your movement on each beat, so her right foot steps back.

On the second beat ('two'), your right foot goes forwards and to the right, in the shape of an upside-down L. Your weight should be on the right foot, your left doesn't move.

On the third beat ('three'), slide the left foot over to your right foot and stand with them together.

On the fourth ('one'), step the right foot back.

On the fifth ('two'), bring the left foot back and to the left, following the backwards and reversed L shape. At the end of this step your weight should be on the left foot.

On the final beat ('three'), slide the right foot back towards the left until they're side by side. You've completed stage one and are ready to step forward with the left foot again. Repeat the above until the music ends or you're out of breath, varying the placement of the feet slightly so you glide around the room a little instead of plodding a small square plot of floor.

Note: This is the basic outline for a traditional, no-frills waltz. The Americans prefer the 'American-style waltz', naturally enough, which involves changing sides, flinging the woman around your head and all that glitzy Hollywood nonsense. For details on that, you'll need another book.

How To ...
Morris Dance

Fuck off.